*Different Cradles,*
*Same Seed*

# Different Cradles, Same Seed

Ruby Alexander

authorHOUSE®

AuthorHouse™
1663 Liberty Drive
Bloomington, IN 47403
www.authorhouse.com
Phone: 1-800-839-8640

First published by AuthorHouse    06/08/2011

ISBN: 978-1-4634-2125-0 (sc)
ISBN: 978-1-4634-2124-3 (dj)
ISBN: 978-1-4634-2123-6 (ebk)

Library of Congress Control Number: 2011909798

Printed in the United States of America

# CHAPTER ONE

I'm in an airplane, leaving Minneapolis to go to Los Angeles for a conference, and began to think of all my grandchildren and what I'd want them to know about me in case I died. Things I want to say and questions I'd like to answer even though they haven't been asked. My heart has been broken many times concerning you. Most of you have lived in my house; some for less than a week, and some for a year or more.

Every time I look at you, I see a miracle. If your parents weren't supposed to be born, then you weren't either. I promised God that I would give your parents back to Him, and I did. So, technically if they belonged to God, everything they possess belonged to Him also; including their seed. All of you that I have adopted, whom I call my Godchildren; Milton (six children), Judi (four children), Pat or Trisha (two children), Charlene (three children), and Warren (three children). You and yours are dear to me; you in me and I'm in you. Even the ones who aren't biological, you have just been had by association. I have asked God to show you the way—not to let you go until you have given your hearts completely to Him. That God will help you live up to the purpose to which you were born. You can't spot my life. I didn't say I was perfect, I said you can't spot my life. I have never been mean or evil. You have never seen anything other than a Christ-like spirit in me. I have loved you all the time and protected you when I could. I used to go out of my way to remember your birthdays and Christmas. Then I made a conscious decision to only give gifts to people who have formed a relationship with me; especially the ones old enough to. I have cried many nights thinking of my babies. You are that. I have held all of you on my breast. You can't imagine the hurt I feel. I don't want to go to my grave, or be raptured without you knowing that if no one else loved you unconditionally, Grandma does. You see, I am responsible

1

for you being here. Maybe the doctors were wrong, but I do believe that God worked a miracle in my body through prayer and I conceived your parents. If I had chosen the three other men I was engaged to, you would have been different people. But divine intervention allowed you to be here. You are not here by chance. I wouldn't have been in Minnesota, so I wouldn't have met Judi, Pat or Charlene. Milton's family wouldn't have sent him to anyone but Alex. I have given you and yours to God also. You are always in my prayers.

When some of you were taken away from me, it tore my heart out. I was, in my opinion, a good grandmother and a good in-law. I never interfered unless I felt your safety was threatened. I made sure you had food and a place to stay. When some of you went to foster homes, I made sure I picked up your mom and we visited.

One day your mom took five of you to another town and I didn't know where you were. I knew you were okay because your other grandparents were involved and I knew they were as concerned about your welfare as I was. They were pastors, as we were. Just because two people come from similar backgrounds, is no indication they can be compatible in a marriage. Your parents were both eighteen when they got married and neither was ready for marriage or responsibility. The children came too fast.

You were not a mistake. I believe that God chose you to be in our family and that He has a plan for your life. You must listen carefully to His directions. He will direct you. It's up to you whether you have a hard time getting to the high road, but to the high road you will get! That's your destiny. You are somebody.

I taught coping skills for over ten years. I can remember telling each class (I would get a new class of adults every two weeks), this story: A farmer will take his prize pig to the State Fair and he can win a blue ribbon because the farmer has bathed him, brushed him down, and whatever else it takes for him to win this ribbon. After he has won it and goes back home, the pig, if left alone will go back to the mud. Someone can clean him up on the outside, but they can't change his nature. His nature is to wallow in the mud."

Only you can change your nature with the help of God. You have a choice. My dad used to say, "If you fall, don't wallow; don't stay down there. Get up and try it again". Know that that kind of life is beneath you.

So I missed a lot of your growing up years. You've been the subject of many of my prayers. Every holiday and birthday I made sure you were taken care of. Then when I couldn't find some of you, I did like AA suggests. In essence, I don't worry about the things I cannot change. I thought, "When they get old enough, they will find me". I made a policy that I wasn't going to be anyone's Santa Claus. When a person, be it family or not, is old enough to form a relationship with me and chooses not to, then I won't stick my nose in their business. When they want me, I'll probably be there.

I want all of you to know that I love you dearly and want only the best for you. But, as some of your parents told me, "My values aren't their values". So I keep my opinions to myself unless asked, but no one can tell me what to pray for. I don't pray that you come to our church. I pray that you come to know and love God. When you have accomplished this, your values will change. I'm only talking to the ones who might need this. There are twenty-three of you who are fourteen and older. None of you are in jail and from what I bear, you are not on drugs. I pray that the hounds of Heaven continue to nip at your heels until you run right into your destiny. The twenty-two younger ones, I'm in their lives. I have visited grand kids in Seattle, Omaha, Detroit, and Jacksonville. All of you are an extension of me.

One Sunday, I informed the congregation that I believed in abortions. I waited for a reaction. The church was quiet. I could feel their uneasiness. Maybe a few were judgmental, but I had everyone's attention. I finally told them how negative thoughts should be aborted when first conceived; use the morning after pill. Even if the thought has been allowed to grow for months, abort it. It is your decision, your right, and your choice to keep that negative thought or kill it. A thought is a seed that will yield off springs somewhere down the line it you don't abort it.

Chapter two, 9:8, in Samuel states that the king's grandson was invited to sit and eat at King David's table. The grandson fell off his chair and lay on the floor and called himself a dog. The king thought him worthy of eating with him, but Mephibosheth, son of Jonathan, the son of King Saul, thought he was nothing.

The king invites us to come and dine, but we say, "I can't because I haven't given up this habit, or I've got something in my life to take care of before I can sit at your table". How are you ever going to get any nourishment in your anemic body if you don't come to the table? Now will you ever get the strength to get well if you don't eat? Unless you allow the king to feed you, you will never gain the strength to turn your life around. Those "I can't" thoughts should be aborted.

Someone told me if I wanted to learn the computer to ask my grand kids. Well, assuming you know how to delete something from the computer, or cancel the command on the microwave, why then don't you try that with your thoughts? Reprogram your subconscious. After you have aborted every negative thought about yourself and others, put a guard (the Word of God and other positive books and tapes), at the door of your mind that will only accept pure, lovely, true, good report thoughts, and reject anything harmful.

There's a song that says, "Come over here, the table is spread, the feast of the Lord is now going on". You have been invited to the table. God would not invite a "dog" to His feast. He deems you worthy. Go and dine with Him so you can grow to maturity; you can be nourished and nurtured. Now during the dinner conversation you can team how better to abort those thoughts and become the person you were born to be. Even a caterpillar knows he was born to fly. The king has fixed a gourmet dinner. He has bid you come and dine. Abort that indecisive thought and choose to let Him prepare the table before you.

Grandma doesn't preach very often, but there are some things I've never had a chance to tell some of you. One day I was trying to videotape a gospel program and couldn't find a clean tape. I found an old Ninja tape and taped over it. Sometimes you want to record something new, but your tape is full . . . tape over it.

You may have hurt many people in your lifetime, sometimes your parents, siblings, teachers, or friends. Whatever the case, no mailer how much you've done in your short lifetime God has made provisions for your forgiveness, and a way for you to forgive. He wipes the slate clean and doesn't even remember your sins anymore The Bible says, "Satan is the accuser of the brethren". It's the negative force who will always bring up your past to you. Record over that accusation. Make sure you have tried to rectify your mistake and forsake it. Ask forgiveness and accept that it is done. When that negative force puts in that tape, eject it. Don't let it play. It's your choice. Don't dwell on how good that joint was or how you felt in the arms of your so-called lover. Don't dwell on how you hate the one who raped you or that incestuous relationship.

If you have to remember anything, remember that drugs kill millions of brain cells, kill many people in car accidents, break up families, leaving widows, widowers, and parentless children, and make people lose jobs, homes and other possessions. Remember that your lover gave you a disease or left you pregnant and is now with someone else, so you are not missing anything.

Thank God that your rapist didn't kill you; that things stopped going on in your family before you lost your mind completely. Talk to someone you trust. If something unseemly is going on, tell someone. Don't keep it to yourself. After that is taken care of, stop blaming yourself. Change that tape. Learn to eject. Tape some positive movies. Dwell on pleasant things. You might have to get some professional help, but as Malcolm X said, "By any means necessary".

In Genesis 32:28 God changed Jacob's name to Israel. If you've been recording Jacob, the trickster, change your tape to record Israel, a prince. Sometimes it's hard to change tapes. Jacob wrestled all night with an angel and said he wouldn't let go until he was blessed or changed. You have to make a conscious effort to reprogram those tapes even if you have to wrestle with your demon until you win.

Write a letter. Read it, cry and then tear it up. I started this when (was fourteen. I used to write a friend who was in the Army, or to some of my pen pals. Tell them everything, but don't mail it. Be your own confidant. There are some things that you should only tell God. He won't betray your confidence. You are writing to a real person and it's a very good outlet.

The only thing I have to leave you is your history, the part I know. I will ask your grandfather, Aunt Pauline and Aunt Birdie to write their part. I want you to know why you feel the way you do and what illnesses you are prone to.

# CHAPTER TWO

My earliest memories are when I was five. I lived in a little two-room, red house on East End Avenue in Chicago Heights, Illinois. The year was 1941. I remember the blackouts and the radio programs "Lights Out", "Bull Dog Drummond", "The Shadow", and "Fibber McGee & Molly". It was so exciting to me to be in the dark with my parents listening to these scary stories them explaining to me that we were in a war and we were practicing what to do just in case the war came to our land.

We had one bedroom, a kitchen and a bathroom. There were three of us in our house, my parents and me. I slept with them. "Every shut eye ain't sleep", is a saying my dad taught me, I think the entire statement is "Every shut eye ain't sleep, and every goodbye ain't gone". I don't know every time my parents had sex, but one particular night I do remember. I also remember how funny I was feeling in my lower parts, and that year I started masturbating I didn't know what you called it, but I know when I felt funny down there that I could stop that feeling by crossing my legs a certain way.

I learned other lessons in 1941. I was going to Sunday school. I saw one of my playmates that happened to be White. She was playing with a doll. I admired the doll and she asked me if wanted it. Of course I did! She gave it to me and I took it to church with me. When I came home I was faced with a stealing charge. The girl's mother had been to our house demanding the doll back. When I got home, Mother marched the doll and me back to the girl's house. I learned not to accept gifts without my mother's permission. At five, I also learned if you swallow a penny you could look for it the next day, if you used the toilet.

I learned that eating too many tomatoes right from the garden can give you hives. My grandmother washed me down with salt and vinegar for the itch. I learned that if your parents were fighting, you might get socked if you cried. I also learned that you shouldn't pull up your mother's dress and show her best friend the black and blue marks on her thighs.

My mother's best friend was my best friend George's mother. I was five and he was four. He's the one who taught me to look for swallowed matter in your stool. We were a team. George, Ruby (the doll girl), and Raymond. Two Whites and two Blacks . . . the East End kids in 1941.

Also in 1941 I went to visit my grandparents in Cleveland, Mississippi. I remember the train ride. It was around Christmas time. I had on a snowsuit. When we arrived at our destination, people looked at me like I was a freak. They had never seen a snowsuit and it was too warm there for this kind of gear.

In my grandparent's house somewhere between Cleveland and Pace, Mississippi, we had a fireplace and a wood-burning cook stove. I don't remember how many moms we had, but the term "shotgun house" fits the bill. You could look straight through the house. At night we would light the oil lamps, build the fire hotter, and put some sweet potatoes in the ashes. I'd help my grandmother churn butter. We would drink our water from a dipper, which we kept in a bucket I learned to prime the pumps so we could get water for washing, cooking, bathing and drinking. We had a barrel on the side of the house to catch rainwater so we could wash our hair. I remember worms and bugs in this water; we had to strain them out.

While I was visiting, we all went to the fields. They tied a pillow slip to my back. I can't remember going to the fields but once or twice. They must have realized that I was more in the way than being of help so they sent me to school with the cousins. It was held in a church. All eight grades in one room. Miss Ann was our teacher at the Pleasant Valley School/Church.

Miss Ann taught me to spell my name when I was five. My grandfather, Simon Perkins, had taught me what he knew . . . Rubie Lee Willie. Well, Willie was not my last name and I got a lick on my hand for every letter in my last name "Williams", I learned to spell my name that day

At five I also learned that you could kill a snake with a hoe. My Aunt Mattie, my mother's youngest sister, took me fishing. She killed that snake. Could it be that at age five my snake phobia began? At this same time I also learned that some older boys could be nasty-.I was on my way to Sunday school, which was about two country blocks from my grandparent's house. On the road, a truck stopped and three White guys about the age of fourteen and fifteen (they looked like men to me) asked me for some pussy. I pretended I had never heard the word. They said, "Awe, she dumb" and drove off. I was so scared I ran to my cousin's house between Grandma's and the church.

I also learned my first Easter speech that year; "What you lookin' at me for? I didn't come to stay. I just come to tell you today is Easter Day!" I learned the value of giving. My dad gave me two nickels, one for church/ God and one for me. I dropped one nickel. I looked for it diligently. When I was satisfied that I wasn't going to find it I said, 'There go your nickel God"! (I called him Dod)!

When I was five, my twelve-year-old Uncle Saul had a twelve-year-old White friend. They had played together since babies. Big Ma helped to raise him. When the plantation owner's son became twelve he informed Pa Simon, Big Ma and Uncle Saul that Saul could no longer call his friend by his first name, but had to call him Mister Charles. Saul cried and said he couldn't do that. He was shipped out of Mississippi to Chicago Heights, Illinois that same week.

My grandfather continued setting traps for rabbits, squirrels, possums and coons. He would set his line out for fish. Every morning he'd go out to see if his night was fruitful. He killed hogs and smoked the meat. Big Ma canned vegetables and made preserves. She oiled my skin in butter. We didn't have lotion. We fed the chickens, picked up the eggs, worked the garden, and dried the peanuts (on top of the house). The next thing I remember, and I was still five years old, we all left Mississippi to go to East Chicago Heights. I can't remember how we got there.

My mother taught me another valuable lesson about stealing. My aunt had moved from her house at 1000 Lexington in East Heights to 1244 Wentworth in Chicago Heights. A grocery store was right across the street. Something got in me and I stole a Twinkie. I was crazy enough to take it home. Well, my mother, after questioning me, marched me back over there after spanking my behind real good and made me give the Twinkie back to the store owner. I had to tell him I had stolen it and apologize to him. It taught me not to steal and I hate Twinkies to this day. She gave me a value, which eventually became my own value. At five I learned not to eat green apples from the tree. Let them ripen or you will get the flux (Southern for diarrhea).

I went to First Union Baptist Church, which was right next door to our house on Lexington. I heard a sermon on faith. It convinced me that locking the door was a lack of it. After my grandparents went to bed, I went and unlocked the door. We slept all night unharmed with the door unlocked. My grandparents weren't too happy with me. You must remember this was 1941 in a small town of about 5,000 people. People didn't just get scared in 1999; they've been scared down through the years.

I learned my first Christian song there. Willie Iron was the choir director. Pilgrim's Journey to the tune of O' Danny Boy. "I must go forth unto a pilgrim's journey along the strange and dimly hidden road". In 1941 many of our men went to the Army and the women went to the war plants. I don't know why my father didn't go into the Army. Maybe because he was thirty-two and had a family. Could it be they couldn't find him? I know that he wouldn't take us back south with him. Something happened when I was six months old and Dad had to get out of Belzonia, Mississippi in a hurry. I heard tales of him being a cut-up in his day, bootlegging, etc. Every year he would sneak back in to see his family. So maybe they were looking for Sam and he was known as Murphy. He worked at a chemical plant so maybe he was exempt.

Murphy was a fighter when he was young. He had a fight with some tavern owners. The three of them went to the hospital and he went to jail. He changed drastically when I was nine. In 1945 I lived at 1421 Lowe Avenue. Renting from the Piazza's. One day in Junior High School in Science Class I saw a picture of a hand with a rash on it. It looked hideous. It had such an impact on me that the next day my hand had the same kind of bumps. They stayed on my hand for several hours.

I had experienced not being able to walk for several weeks because my arch had fallen. I was taken to a "foot doctor". We had three Negro doctors in our town. One was medical, one a dentist, and one female foot doctor. She worked on my feet and about a month later had a nervous breakdown. I was thirteen and it made an impression on me. One day I knew I was going to be late for school. I didn't want to lie so I thought "my arch is down, my arch is down". Before I got to school, I was actually hopping . . . it was an excused tardy.

One day at work, two gunmen came in and robbed us. Half an hour after they left I broke out with "measles". I went to the emergency room of our nearest hospital because my boss had never had measles and he was scared. I was diagnosed with Milieu. My nervous system had gone awry. They treated me and I had to have a special cream to deal with the very small pimples on my hands and face.

These three things have made me realize that most of my sickness is in my mind; that if I could make myself sick, then I should be able to make myself well. So I have spent my lifetime talking to my body, my mind, my emotions and pulling them under control. Therefore, I am very seldom ill for long. Usually two days in bed cures me.

I was so healthy at work I had to create some days I could use to take off. I don't believe in saying I'm sick when I'm not. I don't want to claim that, because words are very powerful. So when I had an extremely difficult class at work, I signed out that night for a day or two of EML—Emotional Leave. Sometimes I would be accident-prone. I'd break a little toe on a chair when walking barefoot, or would spill hot grease on me when taking bacon or sausage from the oven. (I hate to fry bacon or sausage (or anything) so I bake it. It saves time too, you can put it in the oven while you shower).

It was the first time (at five) I remember seeing my grandmother and grandfather. Big Ma, as I called her, Miss Lue as my grandfather and her step kids called her, and Muh as Uncle Saul called her, was Pa Simon's third wife; his other two had died. Technically, she was my step-grandmother, but I didn't and don't know what that means heartwise. I have been blessed to have good parents and grandparents in my life . . . biologically and otherwise.

Big Ma had never had any children of her own. She and Poppa adopted Saul when he was a baby. She married Poppa after his second wife died. The children were teenagers. My grandmother, mother and her sibling's mother had died in childbirth after six children. He married again and she died after five years. Big Ma stepped in and when I was born she and I became inseparable.

The only conflict she and I had was about me sucking my arm . . . not my fingers or thumb, my left arm, about six inches above my wrist! It had a dark spot on it. Anyone could suck a finger. I have always been unique. I don't remember when I realized this and can't remember anyone teaching me this. Big Ma put red pepper, quinine, and chicken manure (at least that's what she told me) on my arm. Nothing stopped my addiction to my arm until a few months before my tenth birthday.

Big Ma was 5'1" and weighed one hundred seventy pounds. She had asthma. She had lo sleep on three pillows at night and she snored really loud. She and Poppa slept in the same room but not in the same bed. When I stayed with them I slept in her bed. Both beds had big feather mattresses. She taught me how to make up the bed by fluffing up the feathers.

Poppa dipped bitter garret snuff and had a spit can near his favorite chair. He emptied his own cans. We also had a slop jar. That was our nighttime toilet since the main relief place was in the back of the house (called an outhouse). Oh, I remember the stench! Now I can sit for an hour reading in my bathroom, but back then I did what I had to do quickly and left.

Big Ma didn't straighten her hair. She wore it washed and water-waved (water, grease and brushed). I think she ordered dresses from Sears and Roebuck, alt that she didn't make that is. She had a few Sunday dresses. Church was the only place you had to dress up for.

Big Ma had beautiful tan skin and a pleasant face. Our house was always peaceful and homey. We laughed, talked and ate those roasted yams and peanuts. Poppa would rock me in his rocking chair and make up little songs to sing to me. I found myself doing that for your parents and many of you.

I watched Big Ma make lye soap, flour starch, and crackling (baked bacon skins and fat). We boiled white clothes in a big pot on a fire in the yard. We had a big alfalfa field in the back of our house. I thought it was just for the animals, now I'm drinking it as tea.

I helped to slop the hogs and milk the one cow we had. They said she was mine, and we named her Jersey. (How original—she was a Jersey cow). We washed dishes and poured the dishwater out of our back door a little to the side. In the morning the worms would have come above ground. We would pick them up and place them in a container so Poppa could set his fishing lines. We would wash our glassware, silverware, dishes, and then pots and pans. We boiled water to scald them and dried them with a clean flour sack bag. Many of these habits were used in the South, but brought to East Chicago Heights.

We bought flour, meal, rice and sugar by the sack or barrel. I'm sure we ate plenty boweevils. Did you know if you put rice, grits or oatmeal in a large amount of cold water, the boweevils and other undesirables would float? You pour that off and start with fresh water.

I learned to snap beans and pick greens and to hang clothes up on a line so the sun could finish bleaching them white. In Mississippi, my grandfather sold animal pellets to mail-order houses. Because he was a sharecropper, he had to make money in other ways. His house was provided on the plantation. He could go to "town" and buy things on credit and pay for it when the crop was in. They got paid once a year (I think). When they got paid they owed most of it to the stores that had extended them credit. If their children, who had escaped the plantation, hadn't sent them money from time to time they would have been destitute.

We quilted. I could only cut out pieces and maybe do a running stitch. I'm sure they did my work over, but they taught me to work. I helped make biscuits, cakes, flapjacks, etc. I licked the bowls. I don't know why we weren't food poisoned. Maybe our systems were accustomed to no refrigeration and raw eggs and milk. We drank clabbered milk that I think was closely related to what we call yogurt now. I know we had a smokehouse where the meat was smoked and kept. The fruits and vegetables were canned and put in a cellar dug several feet down lined and covered with wood and brush.

They also ordered "Biddies" (baby chickens) from a mail-order house. I sort of got attached to them because I saw them from the baby to the table. We ate chicken feet, and even used the intestines to fish with. Carp, suckers, grinners, (fish) etc. will bite at anything. When one of the baby chicks died the kids on our plantation would have a funeral. One of the guys would be the preacher. We'd pray and sing, put the chick in a box and bury it. We'd do the same for dogs and cats. I don't know about dogs, but cats were suppose to keep snakes away . . . probably small ones. Even though the house was shabby, it was clean. Our floors were whitewashed with lye soap and hot water. Our porch was as clean as the rest of the house. We swept our yard also.

Our nearest neighbor was two country blocks away. The alfalfa field was behind us. The barnyard was on the left, and the garden was on the right. A ditch was in front of the house. Three planks were laid across it for a bridge. I hate to think now what else was in there beside crawfish. Across the road were woods where Poppa used to hunt and fish. About one mile past the garden was a road to get to the creek without going through all the woods. That's where my Aunt Mattie and I would go fishing. On the way there we would see dirt daubers; they rolled up stinky stuff in little balls and push them down the roads.

About two miles past the barnyard and church was a larger body of water. Many of the people on the plantation would get in a wagon pulled by a horse and make a day of mudding. We would use a hoe and stir up the bottom of the creek and fish would come to the top of the water. Other critters would also come to the top and we'd clear the water (run).

My relatives had strange nicknames such as Cooter, Duck, Tux, Toad, Rabbit, and Conch. Some of them I didn't know how they became a relative. We had cousins, aunts and uncles galore. I think we just had to put a handle on an adult's name. We were not allowed to call an adult even by their nickname. They were Cuttin' (cousin) Rabbit, Cuttin' Roseanna, etc.

Pa Simon (Poppa, as I called him) was reported to be a Geechee, which is a derogatory name. He was really a sea Islander whose parents lived off the coast of South Carolina. He was maybe 5'2", medium-brown skinned with a southern foreign accent. His speech was singsong twang . . . Richard Pryor tone. I never heard him say a curse word though. He ruled his house quietly. He kept a bottle of homemade peach rum by his bed, but he only drank it when he was sick; not often. He wore his union suit (long-drawers) from late September to early June after he moved to Chicago Heights. Poppa got a job with the CNI Railroad. He worked there for over fifteen years before he retired in 1959. They forced him to retire; he worked past retirement age. He died while I was pregnant with Barton in 1960. In retrospect, Poppa was ladies' man. We had a family of cousins and aunts to move to East Chicago Heights right after Poppa and Big Ma moved. They were from the same plantation. Well, when my grandmother died suddenly, he married this lady, who had been in my life for years, several months later.

I lived in Chicago Heights, which is two miles from East Heights. I spent most summers and many weekends during the school year with Big Ma and Poppa. One Friday night in 1946 she called my father and asked him to bring me out to spend the night with them. Since it was late, my dad said he'd bring me out in the morning. By morning she was dead. I would have been in bed with her.

There are two phobias I had. One is the fear of snakes and the other of dead people. I have practically conquered my fear of the dead, but snakes are still a problem. Big Ma finally cured my arm sucking. I was so afraid she would wake me up spanking my arm, I quit cold turkey. Ten years of hard core addiction is difficult to break. That made me think of the law of gravity and how planes use lift and thrust to fly. My fear of spankings was greater than my addiction and I had no withdrawals. Lift and thrust defied gravity; my fear defied my addiction.

Big Ma was the first person I had lost who was close to me. I grieved, but I can't remember anyone really meeting my emotional needs. No one knew how I loved and missed my grandmother. It never came up that she was a step-grandparent. She had been my protector. One day my Aunt Mattie sent me to the store with a dollar. I lost it. Aunt Mattie was trying to spank me, but Big Ma got between the strap and me and started crying. Oh how I loved that woman. I didn't understand death, but I knew I wouldn't be seeing her again until Heaven. So I was determined to go there. The last time I saw her at church, she had sung a Dr. Watts hymn, "I know I am a child of God, although I move so slow". So I was sure where she was going and I had to meet her there.

This warm loving woman had three great loves in her life; Saul, her other adopted son George, and me. Others just grieved, but we three grieved and bonded. Saul was in his senior year of high school. Had Big Ma lived, she would have been proud of her son and grandkids, and of her granddaughter and her great grand kids. George was lost without Big Ma; no one gave him the love and guidance that he needed so he died relatively young.

Simon Perkins and Mary Range had six children, two sons and four daughters. My mother, Gussie, was the third oldest daughter born on November 11, 1916 (she thought it was 1915 until she tried to get her social security). Mary was full-blooded Indian. I always thought they were half White, but her sisters never talked about it. My Aunts Mattie Range Early and Georgia Range Wilson, and Uncles George and Joe Range, Senior, were all light-skinned and had straight black hair. They were my biological grandmother's siblings. The females birthed no children and Grandma Mary died in childbirth after having six children.

Gussie was pretty and she knew it. She married Murphy Williams. She looked more White than Black when she was younger and he was jet black and handsome. She might be the reason he had to leave Mississippi in a hurry. I called Gussie "Muh Dear" until I went to college. I don't know why I stopped because all my friends called her "Muh Dear" until she died.

Great Grandma Gussie and Great Grandfather Murphy were very passionate. They loved deeply and fought furiously. Most of the things I'm telling you are from observation and hearing stuff when I wasn't suppose to. Children in my day were to be seen and not heard. You didn't get into grown peoples' conversation. You could get snuff skeeted in your eyes if you forgot. You never disagreed with your elders; you'd be calling them a liar. Remind me to tell you about the time that I wanted to kill Aunt Leatha.

One day after we had moved from East End to 1421 Lowe Avenue I asked Muh Dear if I could go to the movies. I loved to go to the movies for the popcorn (movie popcorn tasted better to me then) and for the air conditioning. This was July 4th and extremely hot. I saw a double feature twice. I was about to leave and I saw my cousins Carol and Burnet come in with my aunt. Their mother, Della Perkins Hughes had died from childbirth complications in 1937. This day the kids were with Aunt Arrabelle (Baby) Perkins. I went back in and saw the pictures again. When I got two blocks from my house the kids said my mother was looking for me and she was mad. I ran home, got out of my clothes and into bed. Mother came in and promptly started whipping me and screaming and hollering. I was really scared because this was out of character for her. My dad got her off of me and told me she was scared something had happened to me. Four times in my life she spanked me . . . the doll incident, the Twinkie, the movies, and once when I played hooky in the third grade. One of my "aunts" caught me waiting on the kids walking home for lunch so I could join them and be home on time. She took me to my house and I got it!

Well, the summer when I was ten, I advised my mother to leave my dad because they fought all of the time. Dad was so jealous of her. Reportedly, she danced with Redd Foxx at the Black and Tan Tavern on 17th Street in the Heights. Dad worked at Victor Chemical from about 1941 to 1976. He would go punch in and punch right back out when he was on the 11 p.m. to 7 am. shift. He wanted to catch his wife cuttin' up.

I don't know if he ever did catch her, but I do know she had plenty of admirers. She would leave him after a fight and stay gone for a few weeks. Most of the time she took me with her. She would go to Poppa's house in East Heights or to her cousin's in Chicago Proper. One time she went to Youngstown, Ohio, with other relatives. She stayed about a month. When she got back Dad had moved Miss Emily in; he said so she could take care of me. Someone must have told Muh Dear. She came home. Miss Emily was on the backside; Dad was in the front. Muh Dear got in the bed and

Dad was in the middle of these two women. Finally Miss Emily decided to get out of there. When she got outside she threw a brick through the window . . . honest y'all! Well, they were okay for awhile. I went to Brownie Scout camp. I came home and Mother was in jail and Dad's eye was cut. They had tussled. He fell and cut his eye on the sidewalk. They took them to jail. She had told them if she ever went to jail she would leave for good. She did. We went home to Poppa's. That didn't last long. My father took care of his family. He worked, cooked, cleaned and as he said, he could do anything a woman could do, but have a baby.

Somehow he maneuvered me back home. He asked me if I wanted to stay with him and I said I wanted to stay with both of them. He said I should stay with him because Muh Dear would marry again, it would be the man's house and he could put us both out. On the other hand, if he married, if it didn't work out, he could put her out and get someone else.

While we were adjusting to life without Mother, Dad stopped drinking and dramatically went and laid his head on the railroad tracks and wanted to die. (I wonder, since he was so full of life). Somehow, the story circulated but Muh Dear had made up her mind and no such antics would deter her.

Miss Lottie lived across the street on Lowe Avenue. She knew Daddy's plight and she told Dad about her daughter who had two children and was divorced. They needed a place to stay. She would live with us and take care of me, cook and clean in exchange for room and board for the three of them. So I met Miss Daisy Lee, Mary and Herbert. I am ninety percent sure that nothing went on between Daddy and Miss Daisy Lee. Mary was three years older than I was and Herbert was my age.

Miss Daisy was a good mother and a great cook. One day she cooked kidneys and hot rolls. As the kidneys were browned, she would put them up on the top of the oven. The burners were on the right and the oven was on the left, like a two-oven stove. Mary and I would take a kidney and a hot roll as we left the kitchen to go outside. Those kidneys were so delicious. Stolen fruit must have been good—we couldn't wait till supper. I don't understand it . . . I hate kidneys. They smell and taste like pee.

Miss Lottie made Dad acquainted with a female minister who changed his life. Reverend Stevenson somehow got my dad to quit drinking by telling him that my mom would come back to him if he quit. You see, she had started dating a preacher. So, from the time I was ten until I was twenty, he never drank. That was a change because our house was the gathering place for the drinking community. He had house parties. Miss Daisy would cook and he would provide the drinks. This went on for about six months, until Reverend Stevenson came into our lives.

Mary, Herbert and I had a room in the very back of the house. There was only one way out; it was really the front. We had a peek hole where we could look into one of the bedrooms. We saw things . . . a lady and her boyfriend in bed. I tell you this to let you know that I was a typical child and that I have been there. I drained a beer can. Ick! It tasted like vomit. I'm glad I didn't like it. They scared us—bananas and whiskey could kill you. In the middle to late forties, they had a drink called Singing Sam. It was clear whiskey. Dad had many bottles. I bet he was making money bootlegging. He was a character who told jokes and did a dance called the Alligator, which he wouldn't allow children to see . . . probably X-rated.

Dad went to Christ Soul Saving Station which was having services in my Great Uncle George's basement on Wentworth Avenue. Dad got religion. He stopped drinking and went to church twice a week and on Sundays. Before I knew it, he was a Deacon. Because of his dramatic change, many people visited the church . . . even people who didn't believe in women preachers or in a spiritual church. I didn't say "spiritualist" because they didn't do seances (I don't think). She would "read" you, tell you things about your past and your future. She told Dad that Mother was coming back to him. He towed the line for nine years, but she never rejoined him. They were friendly, but the only thing they had in common was me.

Dad never left Mother's family. Her siblings loved him and her parents did also. So they came to church to see Dad in action. Then he got this great call to preach. Everyone in the family came to hear him, but mother. He preached about Zacheus who went up in the tree to see Jesus. This beautiful, Black, strong man was sweating like a winning horse. He hacked, sing-songed, and wiped pouring sweat. Finally, my Big Ma rescued him with a Dr. Watts hymn. People moaned and shouted. Dad sat down. He later told us that he had gotten old Zac up that tree and didn't know how to get him down. He stuck to being a Deacon after that. He told me this saying, "Do what you can and don't try to do what you can't, be what you are, and don't try to be what you ain't. If you're a tadpole, don't try to be a frog. Stay in the water and keep off the log" The Bible says it like this; "Make your calling and election sure". He was quite the comedian.

I grew up in a Catholic town. I was told that in many families the oldest son was expected to be a Priest, whether it was his calling or not. There are many doctors, teachers, preachers, etc., who are not "called" to that profession. That could be the cause of the shipwrecks many of these people have. Dad was not called to be a preacher.

Miss Daisy Lee and her kids moved across the street when Dad sent for his sister Leatha from Belzonia, Mississippi. She looked like a female Murphy . . . not ugly by any means. Medium length hair, two shades lighter and shapely. She was countree! With a little stutter . . . especially when she got excited.

My first encounter with her was her braiding my hair in what seemed like a thousand braids (which is now fashionable in the 90's) to send me to Sunday school. I cried and Miss Daisy Lee took it down to straighten and curl it.

One day Aunt Leatha sent me to the store to get some tepentine. I was this northern girl going to the store and saying real proper; "May I have a bottle of tepentine"? The two White store clerks looked at me. Then they began to ignore me and talk to each other. They told each other, "Those Black folks talked differently than Whites so maybe she mean turpentine'". I never forgot the pronunciation.

The next incident was when she asked me a question, "Where does so and so live"? I said, "I don't know Aunt Leatha". She said, "You don't know? You better say you don't nome!" I was washing dishes and had a large black iron skillet in my hand. I raised it to hit her. My sister, Doris stopped me. She must have told Daddy Murphy, as she called him, and in a week he got Aunt Leatha an apartment next door. In about a month, Dad married Miss Mary, a neighbor who had a son named James.

He was true to his word. If one didn't work out, he would get someone to care for me. I don't know whether Dad got a divorce from my mother, but I know Miss Mary got a divorce from her husband. They had a civil ceremony. Reverend Stevenson didn't like common law marriages.

I was twelve and James was fourteen. We went to church as a family. Reverend Stevenson gave me a thirst for the Word of God. We had a scripture learning contest. How many words, the longest and shortest books, etc. She kept me searching the scriptures. One day she was praying for me and prayed about my mother. I started crying and she said I had gotten religion. I was just sad about my mother.

Dad was a loving father, but he demanded I not see my mother and stepfather. I had to pass their house on 16th and Portland to go to church and I'd stop by. If I was late, he questioned me and spanked me. Several times I was on my way to his Sunday school and stopped off at the little storefront church on 15th and Portland where Mr. Willie was teaching Sunday school. I enjoyed their Sunday school but I couldn't attend. Then my mother and Mr. Willie left town and went to Omaha, Nebraska. We corresponded by mail. She was there for several months until she moved to Chicago proper.

In those years, I fell abandoned. My mother left me for a man. I think these are the things that made me maternal. I befriended anybody, who was down-and-out or people no one liked. When I changed churches, I would bring the two oldest people at our church home for dinner on Sundays. I mothered everyone and in turn, I was mothered. I gave what I needed.

My period started when I was three months into my tenth year. The first month I wore toilet paper. I didn't know what was going on. (We didn't have sex education in school). This was 1946 so there were no sanitary napkin advertisements. Tampons were not invented yet (I don't think). My Aunt Leatha saw my soiled clothes and proceeded to tell me how to care for myself. We tore up old white sheets and towels. She made a belt from a sheet and showed me how to wear rags during my period. I was told to use a pail with a top on it and to put the soiled rags in this pail with cold water. They soaked until my period was over and then washed on a scrub board, in a number three tub outside of the house, until they were snow white. I did this for over a year. My mother brought me some Kotex (the largest box I had ever seen) and a safety belt when she realized what I had been doing. She was appalled that I was wearing rags and that I had started so early. Aunt Leatha taught me not to take a bath during my period and that I shouldn't get my head or my feet wet, especially. I was told that my pores were opened and I could catch consumption (TB). I could take a limited sponge bath, using a wash pan, and sponging off necessary parts.

One day I went to visit Mr. Willie's parents and his unmarried siblings. I must have been permeating the place because his sister Hazel took me in the bathroom and showed me how to wash myself and change my pads. She also gave me some deodorant. Each lesson I was taught was a one-time thing. I was an apt student, eager to learn and seldom forgetful.

I was about twelve. I had been offending people one week out of the month for two years. No wonder in Bible days the women were isolated for a week.

When Dad married Miss Mary, she kept me supplied. I couldn't have asked for a better stepmother. When I wanted to change churches, she and James went to church with me. By that time, the little storefront had built a church across the street on 16th and Portland. I had visited the tent on 16th and Center where my Uncle Rufus and Aunt Baby Perkins later built a house.

I was twelve and all three of us we were seeking for the Holy Ghost, (we didn't know any better, He wasn't lost). We were in revival and James and I would fast until after service for this experience. All three of us, during the month, received the Holy Spirit. Miss Mary was the zealous one. She told Daddy that he was on his way to hell. He was still smoking and who knows what other rules he was breaking, because our new church had a lot of rules.

I loved it because I was a frustrated nun. I loved the discipline. I would have been a nun, but I wanted to marry and have children. Pentecostal was the closest I could get to that disciplined life. We couldn't do anything . . . no makeup, no movies, ball games or even play ball. Sleeves and hems had to be a certain length, etc.

Well, when Miss Mary told Dad he was going to hell and began shouting, he promptly got his gun and threatened to shoot us. Here we are eating up his food and living in his house and telling him he was going to hell. So he forbade us to go to church. We were back at Reverend Stevenson's. When Dad worked from 3 p.m. to 11 p.m., Miss Mary would let me go to Portland Street. I had to leave at 10:15 p.m. so I could be home and in bed by 11:00 p.m. She was my co-conspirator.

I don't know whether he would have shot her. He never hit her, but when he was with Mother, I heard he had beat up three tavern owners on 17th Street. They took him to jail and then to the hospital . . . his bluff on us was good!

This church was the best thing that had happened to me. All of the older women mothered us. I needed that. They set rules and I complied. I was fourteen when I got my first formal dress. We had a banquet. My dress was chartreuse. I probably wore a size thirteen. I had a bust size 34a. My dress showed a little cleavage. One of my mothers had brought a large laundry pin. She folded my formal over and pinned it. I sat through the banquet with this pin in front of my dress. I'm sure I must have been embarrassed but I can't remember feeling like that. I wanted to belong, to fit in so much that I would take it.

Most of the people there were families. They all knew my background. My mother had taken their assistant pastor from his wife. So, I'm the bad girl gone good. I had to be extra good to be accepted (No one told me this. It was my perception). Somehow, I never got a complex. I was friendly and adhered to all the rules. If you liked me, good. If not, so be it. I could never spend the night with anyone other than Mother (and the pastor's family once). Any of my friends could spend the night with me. My dad's philosophy was, "I don't know what's happening at their house, but I know what's happening here, so they can come over here".

Murphy, my dad, was strict. I went to church if the pastor's family picked me up and brought me home. He had to hear them say "goodnight" to me. I had to be home within a half-hour after school was out until I was halfway through my senior year. Then I had forty-five minutes. Miss Mary and James finally quit going to church at all, but she helped me go. We would tease her. We would talk about Dad and he'd get her in the bedroom and she'd tell him what we had said. Dad was good.

Dad kept going to Reverend Stevenson's church until I graduated from high school and went to live with my stepfather's sister, Aunt Flo. He had told me that I was grown at eighteen. I graduated June 15 (his birthday), 1954. I was eighteen the next day. I moved with Aunt Ho. They had no such rules. You were a kid until you got married. So I had left Dad and gone into a stricter home!

Aunt Ho was ten years older than I was and she had three children. She belonged to the same denomination, but she didn't have all the rules. I could wear a little lipstick and we went to drive-in movies. Her husband's cousin took me to the Ice Capades on a date and I had to take her ten and six-year-olds along as chaperones.

Aunt Ho got me my first job out of high school. I worked as a cashier where she worked on Roosevelt Road and Kedzie. We lived at 1421 Kedzie, just two blocks from work. I went to National Cash Register School to learn how to operate that machine. I was good. Aunt Flo was better. I began visualization on this job. I pictured the cash register. I saw myself working it. I would go so fast, I would break the machine.

# CHAPTER THREE

If hatred means a strong dislike, I have hated several people in my lifetime. Daddy, Aunt Leatha, Joe (the roomer who raped me), and nasty old men. Be very careful whom you allow to live in your house. Dad was a hustler. He made money many ways. He rented rooms to single men. I had two teenage male cousins living there. These cousins got jobs and helped out. J.W. bought a Model-T Ford in 1947 and we had fun riding in it.

J.W. and Alfred had a friend named Joe who also rented a room. I knew Joe when I was a kid on East End. He had a beautiful wife named Miriam. They divorced and he rented a room with us. I was twelve and he was about twenty-five. I had a boyfriend named Sidney. He lived at the end of our block. He was an American Cuban with jet-black straight hair and big, big, juicy lips. Sidney was fourteen. Dad had bought a gun (so he said) to keep Sidney away from our house. I was scared of Daddy. Joe told me if I didn't let him have sex with him, he would tell Daddy he caught me with Sidney. The pain, humiliation, and anger rolled into hatred. He raped me three times before one of our lady roomers, who came to us several years ago when the racetrack opened up, caught him. She told Daddy. He whipped me and put Joe out for about four months.

I was determined I wouldn't cry. I was so angry. Why didn't he use that gun he had bought for Sidney and shoot Joe? Why not protect me? Why think I was fast? He used a belt and tried his best to make me cry. I refused. The hurt was nothing compared to the feelings I was formulating in my spirit against him and men. In four months Joe was a frequent visitor at our house again, but he never bothered me and he never apologized. It was never mentioned by anyone again until one night I was asleep on the couch. When the racetrack opened I gave up, my bed to the couple who rented my room. My dad came in with a flashlight. I woke up with one of my legs on the back of the couch and the other on the floor. He had a flashlight looking at my private parts. I took my foot and tried to kick the living daylights out of him. I tried to kick him in the next room. I made so much noise I woke the house. He said he was trying to see if Joe had really raped me. I don't know, but I was determined that no one else would rape me. They might kill me, but they wouldn't rape me. Don't take anything away from me. Not even a penny. I hate a thief and Joe had stolen my virginity.

To rub it in, I went to a church where virginity was preached. Father LittleJohn would come to the church and randomly ask girls, "Daughter, are you a virgin"? Or he would ask a man who was old enough if he was married. I don't know how many girls lied, but everyone he asked was a virgin. Strangely enough he never asked me. I guess I was smart enough not to get n his prayer line.

I had to see Joe in this little town of 35,000 people very often. I was raped that summer and that fall I experienced a deeper relationship with the Lord. I had to deal with my hatred. I would give it to God and then I'd see Joe. Then he became a preacher in a Baptist Church. His pastor brought him to our church and let him preach. He preached all over the Bible. Maybe I was overly critical because I had not really forgiven him. He never asked me to forgive him. I had to do it whether he asked me to or not. It was only hurting me. It took me several years to be able to look at him with something other than revulsion. Somehow, he paid. I don't know how, but life is like that.

In the meantime, I have "paid" for many years. I told every boyfriend I had about Joe. I let them know that sex was out of the question, that I had been raped and I didn't want any junk. I kissed and really enjoyed kissing. I never got overwhelmed until I was safely inside my house. After I got married, two specialists told me I couldn't have babies. My womb was infantile. Do you think it was injured in that rape?

I hated my father for how he had treated my mother and how he just took me from her. I had a love/hate relationship. I hated him because he didn't at least beat Joe up like he did those tavern owners, because he punished me after that whipping by keeping me away from church for three months at a time, and made me go to Reverend Stevenson's church. He thought I was "good" because he kept a tight line on me. He allowed me to write my own excuses. I could have taken off school any day and write my own excuse. "If you want to kill a dog, you can always find a stick". I was good because I wanted to be, not because I had to be. There was a story about a woman who was so jealous of her husband that she dropped him off at work and picked him up. This man had a twelve-year affair on his lunch hour. People find many ways of doing what they want to do. He didn't trust me and I resented that. He chose a boyfriend for me. The fellow was cute, almost pretty, but country. He was slight in build and the color of coffee with cream, not Boston coffee. Maybe if he had not been chosen I could have liked him. But he didn't belong to my church and that was against the rules.

This fellow finally married someone else and they had five babies. She lost her mind. He was very whorish. I could say "ladies man", but that's a contradiction. In my opinion a "ladies man" is a man who loves and protects ladies. Not one who tries and succeeds in getting into a bunch of silly, lonely and desperate women's panties.

Aunt Leatha was mean to me. When she was diagnosed with cancer of the uterus, I had to sit with her after the surgery. She had the worst odor several years before she was diagnosed. Uncle John smelled just like her. He was a nice old man. He bought her many nice things. He treated her like a queen.

Well, the saying goes "Be careful how you treat a person, because they might have to wipe your behind before you die". I've always thought that would be punishment for the wiper as well as the wipee! Anyway, Aunt Leatha was so sick, critical. I sat there all night and heard her groans. I forgave her. I knew then that there was a difference between not liking a person and not loving them. I loved her and didn't want her to die. I had to go away to sing with our church that Sunday evening. My sister, Alberta sat with her. I rushed back, but Aunt Leatha was dead. I was glad she didn't die on my shift. I was still terrified of dead people.

Uncle John wanted to give me her white fur coat and her diamond watch. I refused both of them. The main reason was my terror. The next is my theory, "If don't want you, I don't want anything you've got", If I didn't like her in life, why should I profit from her death? I was young, hut I was "old".

Because I was a big girl, when I was a freshman in high school my measurements were 36-26-43½; nasty old men tormented me. I inherited a switch from my mom. People thought I was walking that way on purpose. It had something to do with how our thighs hit together. One nasty Bishop, after our entertainment committee had done something nice for the out-of-town guest, called me and asked to take me to dinner as a show of appreciation. I was twenty and he was sixty, if a day. He was tall, real black, stately and handsome. I told him that I had a date, but I'd love to go if my boyfriend could go also. He said, "If I had wanted your boyfriend to go, I would have asked your boyfriend to go!" and slammed down the phone.

I guess I was naïve. I thought a Bishop was saved, and that he had good intentions. Some Bishops are saved and some are not. Know this . . . that a tree is known by its fruit. You don't have to judge an apple tree. If apples are on the tree, if it looks like an apple and tastes and smells like an apple, by golly it must be an apple. If he acts like a nasty old man, keep your eyes open, be aware, he just might be one. No matter who he is, a doctor, lawyer, preacher, teacher, friend, or relative; get him off your back quickly.

The same goes for nasty old women. They can molest you, female or male. No one is exempt. Your virtue is all you have. Choose wisely. Make sure you give no one a stick to use against you.

# CHAPTER FOUR

A snake healed me once. When I was five I was running in an alley and fell on a large piece of glass. I cut my thigh. I could see the white flesh. It hadn't started to bleed yet. I jumped up and ran to the adults. My Great Aunt Mattie took some soot from the stovepipe and put it on my cut; she said to stop the bleeding. My mother took me to Dr. Martin, our only Negro doctor in town at that time. He said he would have to stitch me up without painkillers. I wouldn't let him do it but I let Dr. Blair, a White doctor do it (ain't that nothing!); five years old and already conditioned that White folks can do it better! I screamed and hollered so loud with all five stitches that Mother was ashamed to go out through the waiting room; he let us use the back door. She almost carried me. I was in so much pain. Having babies is the only thing I can compare this pain to.

In about a week or so I was to go back to get the stitches out. She had to wait on me because I could hardly walk. I worked her. On the day the stitches were to come out, we were going to the doctor who was about four blocks away if we crossed the field from East End to and Halsted, across the railroad tracks. I was barely making it . . . just hobbling. Mother was practically carrying me. All of a sudden she yelled "SNAKE!" and I ran so fast and didn't stop until I was out of the field and on the sidewalk about half a block away. I looked back and my mother was bent over in laughter. I looked and realized I was well. We laughed so hard. All the time in the waiting room we giggled. When the doctor finished, we went to the Rio Theater. That snake healed me; fear superseded pain.

When I was a child, the older people controlled us with fear. They told snake stories. Stories about jointed snakes . . . you cut them and they would go back together. A Blue Racer would run after you, on its tail. I was a child so I could imagine the snake up on feet running. The Coach

26

Whip would whistle like a man; catch you and whip you to death. One snake loved to nurse breast milk. These snakes lived under the house and in the loft. You needed to stay near your family to be safe.

If the snakes didn't get you, the mad dogs or the "haints" would. You were in at dark because of the ghost stories. Many stories were told about dead people and wakes. They used lo put a person in the house and watch to see if he came back to life; see if he wakes up . . . WAKE, get it? You might be carrying someone to the graveyard and they would wake up. Or a person sees someone who is dead. They come back with a message to the living. Or, they push the second wife out of the bed.

One man who was over thirty told me that his mom still hits him on the head if he's home after midnight, but he's also the man who bit the dog who bit him, and the one who was the coffee maker in the Army. He washed out the giant coffeepot the night before and turned it over. The next morning he turned it right side up, filled it with water and coffee grinds and boiled the coffee. A man came in and said, "Suicide (his nickname), give me a cup of coffee!" He gave it to him. He drank. In a few minutes his eyes rolled to the back of his head and he fell off the chair dead. Upon investigation, there was a scorpion in the pot.

He also told me how he went mudding once. He reached down and realized he had latched on to a Water Moccasin. He ran with this snake. When they caught up with him, the snake was stiff. He had squeezed it to death. So his mother hitting him, even though she was dead, was just one of those stories.

Fear was heavy in my house. My stepmother, Miss Mary, and I used to sleep together when Dad was working nights, after someone died. One day I had two female relatives spend the night with me. The man next door had died. He died loudly. He had been sick for a few weeks. This particular night he hollered until about 3 am. My window was opened because it was extremely hot. At 3 a.m. this hollering stopped and his families began. I knew he was dead. I was on this couch again and I was scared. I didn't feel as if I could go in to sleep with my Dad and Miss Mary. I don't ever remember experiencing that much fear. I felt his spirit (haint) hovering over me. I was terrified. It was so good when the sun finally came up.

That night my cousins came. We three slept in the full-sized bed with Miss Mary, with a blanket over our heads in eighty-degree weather. We were roasting, but we felt safe. Like an ostrich—head in the sand. Like a ghost, if there is such a thing, couldn't penetrate a blanket, he could get in the house without opening the door, why not under a blanket?

One night a friend in my mother and Mr. Willie's apartment building died. They fought for the backside of the bed . . . not a fistfight, just wrestled. I think Willie won. They swore that the record player, which the friend loved to play, began to play by itself!

I didn't get over that fear until after Grandpa Alex started pastoring and one of his members tricked me. I'm really not good going to the hospital with people. I stay in the waiting room and minister to and comfort the family. When they are comforted and prayed for, they can impart that to their sick family member. You see I pick up on other's pain. If their stomach hurts, so does mine. One little girl, (she's about 4'9") from our church had her first baby. She wanted everyone to be there. I went. She called for me and, reluctantly I went in the labor room. They wanted to do a C-section, but she refused. She was groaning and hollering. Whenever she did, I did also. She was in pain and so was I. I was as loud as she was.

So when Clarence's wife died, I was with the family in the waiting room. Clarence said, "Come here Ruby. I want to show you something". I followed him into the room where she had just died. He took me to her bed and said, "I want you to feel this" and dropped her arm into my hand. It was the first lime I had ever touched a dead person. She wasn't cold, but her arm was extremely heavy to be so small. My phobia's gone. I'm not on my head to touch dead folks, but I can go to the toilet at the mortuary alone now. I can help the family choose the coffin and clothes for their loved ones. My dad use to say, "The dead person can't hurt you, but it can make you hurt yourself".

# CHAPTER FIVE

My church sheltered me. I was in it from ten years old. I only listened to Country Western Music. I could only watch TV after I had done my homework and studied four Bible studies. So I didn't know much about Richard Pryor. I was trying to find someone to go somewhere with me. No one was available. I thought, "I'm good company, let me be with me". I took myself out to eat and to a movie. You see, I had relaxed some of the rules of my church. I saw the marquis "Richard Pryor in Concert". I thought this would be great. I paid my fare and got my popcorn. I chose my seat carefully and settled down to see a good movie. Well the first five or ten minutes my mouth was dropped. I was in shock. Then I got so tickled and laughed so loud that the people stopped laughing at Richard and started laughing at me. I had never heard anything in my forty-four years to equal that! I actually didn't know the magnitude of Richard Pryor's humor. We saw Richard, Redd Foxx and Moms Mabley on TV, but they were relatively clean, yet funny. I had never heard a party record. It was extremely funny, but nothing I would choose to go to again.

One day I went to a meeting at the University of Minnesota. Our family was the only Black people there. I had been on a diet and when I stood up, my skirt fell off. It was embarrassing and exhilarating at the same time. My group surrounded me till I redressed. We laughed! I try to be a lady and act refined in most situations, but I lost myself on this occasion.

I became chemically dependent in 1956. I wanted to lose that forty-three and a half hip size so I went to my doctor. He gave me diet pills. I took one in the morning. I wasn't hungry all day. I had plenty of energy and worked up a storm. I couldn't sleep at night. Well, that's not true. I didn't want to sleep at night. I had too much energy to waste on sleep. I existed on about three hours a night. One day my head started hurting at 6 p.m., when it was time for me to go home from work. It hurt until I fell asleep at 2 a.m. When I got up at 5 a.m., I would take my pill. The closer I got to Chicago, the better I felt. I commuted two and one-half hours each way.

I have always been snippet. I say what I want, and since I'm opinionated, I said a lot. Well, I was having sexual problems. My hormones were kicking. I prayed and fasted, but I was still having trouble. One day I talked with two of the mothers of our church and told them how I was feeling. No one could ever blackmail me; my life is an open book. I believe in talking about it so it won't grow. Look at it and deal with it. If you hide it, it will fester and grow. These mothers laughed at my boldness and maybe my assumption that God would take away something He had given us.

These headaches were getting the best of me so I hitched a ride with my boyfriend to the doctor. He gave me six pills and told me to take one a day for six days, to stop taking the diet pills, and to see him in a week. He asked to speak to my boyfriend alone. He didn't tell me what the doctor said until after I was married to Alex. The doctor told him to give me a lot of good loving. Well, those pills took away the headache and every sexual desire I had. I didn't even want to kiss anyone. In fact, the thought repulsed me. I was that way for six months then gradually my desire came back. Then I got married.

I went back and told those ladies what had happened. I don't know whether they believed me or not. The doctor said those pills were not doing that. I don't know what happened, but I do know that I gained the weight back in two months. It took me six months to lose it.

I have a low tolerance for pain, but I was tired of being fat. After babies, I had gained lots of pounds. I had gone from a size thirteen to a size forty-eight, maybe even a fifty-two. My top weight was 348 ½ pounds. I decided I would get a gastric bypass. I had done research. I had observed people who had had this procedure. Two had died, so I waited five years and studied more people. In 1982 I had it done. I was in so much pain. They want you to get up right after surgery. No, they make you get up. How can you get up when your insides are coming out? You just want to lie there until the pain goes away. Give me a pill! I could not have been the nurse I wanted to be. I would probably be in jail for assisted suicide.

When I went into the operating room, my family was the last faces I saw. My youngest was sixteen years old. I really didn't care whether I woke up or not. I was a Christian and had done the best I could do with my family. I think that was the year Barton was in court and we were losing our house. I was tired. Well, I did wake up and I was full of pain. I think I was in the hospital for six days. We had lost our house so Alex, Bretta, and I went to Barry and Mary's house. Byron went to stay at Grandma Gussie's; some of you call her Munner.

I remember Thanksgiving that year. I cooked a Turkey and almost broke my stitches because of lifting. A few of our members at the church left because they felt if we were living right, we wouldn't be going through all of this.

I never got my children guns or weapons for a present. They couldn't look at the three stooges where they play "hit each other. Even many cartoons were violent. I never taught them to fight because I thought instinct would teach them since self-preservation was a law of nature. Their father taught them not to start a fight, but to finish it.

One day after Barton had moved to his house. Two years before, we had bought a house in Barton's name because Alex took a leave of absence from work to work with the church. It was our money, and Barton's name.

Barton was twenty when he and his friend decided to buy a shotgun. Barton shot at his garage from his back porch. The bullet went through his back yard, into his garage, out the backside of the garage, across the alley, through another backyard, and into the kitchen of the people on the next street. A little girl was sitting at the table eating breakfast. Her leg, or thigh, was shattered. After much hospital care and much prayer, she came through. But, and rightly so, they sued our house from under us. Technically, it was Barton's house. They didn't take the house he was living in. They took his "rental" house. Her grandmother was a fellow Christian but she quit speaking to me. I wrote her a letter and told her that we had to show Christ for the two unsaved sons. I hope she forgave me for having Bart before she died. Evidently she held that against me.

I lost 188 pounds. I was down to a size fourteen. I looked okay, but felt bad. I got depressed, then found out that I was lacking vitamins and minerals. I felt weak and had no pizzazz. My body looked good, but my face and neck was looking old. I went on a conscious effort to gain some weight back. I couldn't eat but a little at a time, but I could add another meal. I was skinny for ten years. Then I started moving from a size eighteen, which is ideal for me, to a twenty-two, twenty-four. Now I'm working on a size twenty by eating correctly and exercising, I wasn't a snacker, but that's how I gained my weight back. Now it's a hard habit to break.

When I was a size thirteen, when I got married, I shopped at the Ladies Shop on Halsted Street in Chicago Heights. I have never been name brand conscious. If saw something I liked,

I bought it. The Ladies Shop altered my clothes. They took it up in the bust and let it out in the hips. So I guess I didn't actually wear a thirteen. Now I have looked in my closet and found that I do have very good taste. I just bought what I liked and many times, more than not, it was a brand name.

One day in 1953 there was a flood in Chicago Heights. I had all of Grandpa Alex's letters he had written me from Korea. My dad said he got out of bed and had to swim because the water was up to the mattress. Many southerners like high beds, I know I do. Well, Grandpa Alex's letters went floating by and since there was no love lost between my two favorite men his letters were not Daddy's priority.

I have a very good voice, but have no training. With training I could have been an opera singer. I would say I sing Gospel, but your parents tell me I have no rhythm or soul. I love the Gospel sound, but I can't do those runs. I was in the first "Black Nativity" at Penumbra Theater. I auditioned with a Gospel song, "Because He Lives". I could see that wasn't unusual so I asked him to play "Go Down Moses™"; I was a shoe-in. Theater is hard work. I had to take six weeks off work to do the show. I really enjoyed it, but unless I gave up my job, I couldn't do it again. At sixty-one I might go and get some training. As long as there is breath, it's not too late. So, if you have some ambitions, don't wait.

I have lived a full life, and things I've really wanted to do, I've done. I've put some of my desires on hold to help organize the church. I felt that was my mission until it got on its feet. There was a time when the church hinged on Alex and me. Now God has raised up people to help.

Reverend Stevenson took the young people from her church to Oak Forest Medical Center. We took food and drink there twice a year to serve the seniors and the mentally challenged. We made coffee, sandwiches, and boiled eggs. The recipients were so appreciative that it altered my life for good. I knew this was what I wanted to do with my life. I wanted to help people. So, when Elder Cornelius Jackson became the assistant pastor of our church in Chicago Heights, and took me to Joliet Prison at age fifteen in 1951, I was hooked for life. A team of us went twice monthly to Joliet,

Statesville, or Pontiac Prison. We went to tuberculosis clinics and I was more rewarded than the people we ministered to.

When we moved to Minnesota in 1967 I wrote to Stillwater State Prison and asked them about staffing a ministry. We were allowed to go every fifth Sunday and then every third Sunday. Before we left Stillwater for Sandstone and Duluth Prisons, we were going every Thursday night for a Bible study.

The inmates threw us out of Stillwater. We had twenty-five in our group, about eight Whites and seventeen Blacks. We used a While man's van to get us to prison. The cultural group demanded we not bring any White's back. I couldn't see how I could have a segregated Bible study group so we all went back. The guards were doubled, the cameras were perched, and the tension was high. The cultural group came in and asked us to leave. We left. I am sort of unique. That was so exciting to me.

The following week, I sent the White group up and they kept our Thursday night going as long as they wanted to go. One of the reasons I wanted to go to the prisons in Minnesota was because we have a prison full of minorities even though when I moved here Blacks were about one percent of the Minnesota population. I thought it would be good for the inmates if a Black group came in and saw their faces. We could communicate. I could take their conditions back to the churches and other communities. Grandpa Alex was working 4 p.m. to 12 am. and I couldn't find a church or a pastor to help me. Brother Rout offered and I accepted. Help is help, and he was a brother in the Lord.

Your parents were all involved at one time or another in our prison ministry. On April 7, 1777, each one of your parents was at the opening of the church, except Charlene. I met and adopted her in 1984. I have some beautiful children . . . Michael, Linda, Milton, Debbie, Judy, Pat, Doug, Barton, Carolyn, Charlene, Bobby, Barry, Mary, Bretta, and Byron. Each mate is also my child . . . Cecil, Teresa, Kris, Paula, Tulani and Sharon joined the family later. I also have grandchildren by Christine, Cha'Ron, Paula and Tonnia.

# CHAPTER SIX

I was about ten before I knew where babies really came from. I didn't know how they got out. Maybe I was older than that, because when I was raped it never occurred to me that I might get pregnant. I didn't. Poppa told me that Rabbits found me in a cabbage leaf, and I believed it. The cabbage leaf wasn't in our garden; it was deep in the woods somewhere. Each family has their own story.

We worked hard, played hard and walked everywhere so we were strong physically. Now young people can't walk a mile to school. Can't and won't walk five blocks to church. They have a dishwasher, a washing machine, and dryer. They have no-iron clothes, electricity, microwave computers and cars. So they have little energy and plenty of smarts—whether street or formal school, maybe both.

Cancer, Diabetes, Heart Failure, and high blood pressure run in our family. If you don't smoke or use drugs including alcohol and exercise and eat right, our family can rid ourselves of many of these generational curses.

I learned to do a job well. They were either clean or you had to do them over. You hung your clothes where everyone could see and yours couldn't be dingy. Your panties were hung with the crotch folded in. Men were not supposed to see our unmentionables. To this day my husband has never seen my dirty panties. In fact, I wash my panties out every night.

I had approximately 100 pen pals from the Bud Billikin Pen Pal Club. This kept me from being lonely and took the place of live-in siblings. One night I had a dream. I was passing a hospital when a mummy came out with an ax. He chopped me in half. I felt the pain. I woke up scared. 30 years later I got the interpretation while I was counseling a lady going through a divorce. I had that dream when my parents were going through their separation. I told this lady not to bad mouth her husband. Then the dream came to mind. I was chopped in half because my parents were splitting and I heard negatives about both of these people I loved and my heart was broken. Even though they were splitting up, I was the one torn and had no one there really to help me. I had the pen pals, but I couldn't tell them these personal things about my family. I kept them bottled up. I had not learned to write, read and destroy yet.

Aunt Suzie, Miss Mary's aunt, taught me not to put a fork in the bread when it was served to you. Take it with your hand. She let Miss Mary do it but she corrected me. I was about 13. She wanted me to learn the correct way. I read a lot of etiquette books after that.

I went to Uncle Tom's 95th birthday party when I was 15. He was born in 1858. He was Grandpa Murphy's Great, Great Uncle. I saw him take his last breath about one year later. He lived on 93rd and Wabash in Chicago. I saw my cousin Bubba in a National Guard's uniform. It was my first time seeing him. He flirted and looked good, but when we found out we were going to the same place and that we were cousins, we bonded as relatives who were losing an uncle and a great part of their history.

# CHAPTER SEVEN

I had only heard of welfare or relief. This wasn't a thing that happened in the community I was in. The men worked outside of the homes and women did day work where they cleaned rich women's houses. When I was twelve (1948), the going rate was $25.00 a day. Miss Mary had a science. She was so good and fast, they left the task and the money. She could leave when the job was done. She could do two in one day. She had regulars, so once she did the initial cleaning, she just had to keep it clean.

When I had two parents they were not good for me. When they remarried I ended up with four good parents. Sometimes I think they used me. But many times I used them. I would have two outfits for Christmas and Easter.

Miss Mary and Mother became allies. In fact, one weekend Miss Mary took me to Chicago to be with Mother and they slept in the same bed. Well, they had something in common; they both loved me. Miss Mary didn't even know Daddy when he and Mother were together. So she had no part in the separation. On the other hand, Daddy and Willie never did anything but be cordial to each other. If Willie hadn't been in the picture, he thought she would have gone back to him.

I started baby-sitting at twelve. My first charge was Sylvia. Then I baby-sat for a couple who owned a restaurant on 16th Street. Once or twice, I worked in the restaurant. This was during the times when my dad kept me away from church for three months at a time. I worked to fill the void. I worked in Miss Daisy Lee's restaurant on Wentworth. I learned to make great chili and juicy hamburgers; almost as good as Sloppy Joe's on 16th and Lowe Avenue.

I had a piggy bank and Daddy broke it one day, and used my money. When he paid me the $25.00 back, I took it to Sloppy Joes and bought all my friends some hamburgers. They were big and greasy and soooooo good! After buying candy and other treats, my $25.00 was gone. I can't imagine where it all went because hamburgers were just a nickel and a candy bar was probably a dime.

During high school, I washed dishes at St. James Hospital. I had never seen an automatic dishwasher before. I would go after school and do the dinner dishes. I shudder to think of the germs that were left on the dishes in the greasy spoon restaurants. I never saw an inspector and conditions were less than desirable in retrospect.

I worked in Park Forest at the bowling alley one summer. Blacks back in the fifties were still "Negroes". We couldn't bowl there, but we could set up pins. I gave out shoes. I never let anyone talk down to me. If I wasn't treated right, I just quit. Jobs were easy to find. Then I became a cashier. I worked my way through school with this occupation. I worked at several grocery stores around the Chicago area. I was in a union and all I had to do was call my union steward and he would get me a job.

I was proud to tell people that I never received a short check. I could very well have been classified as a workaholic, but I was just committed to commitment, My dad taught me that my word should be my bond. If I say I'm going to do something, or be somewhere, I could be trusted to do it.

My name and reputation are the only things that are mine alone, and I have to make that positive. When people think of me I want them to say, "She was always the same, never moody, and if she said something, you could put your money on it".

That's why it was hard for me to adjust to Grandpa Alex. Our values were so different. I came from my strict daddy where I had to leave a trail if I ever visited anyone. If I left that person's house, I'd have to tell them where I was going and so on. Well, Grandpa had been on his own since he was fifteen. He didn't have to account to anyone. So, when we were married (after about six weeks), he didn't come home one night and I panicked. He had to be hurt in an accident and in the hospital, in jail, dead, on lying somewhere on the side of a road, bleeding. My low tolerance for pain includes emotional pain also. I don't know which is worse.

Because our family is so fragmented, I started praying that the Lord would "send" me my husband, one who I could live with for my entire life. I was embarrassed to try to explain my family. I had a mother and three stepmothers living at the same time. I had siblings . . . none whole, but six half and eleven step. My two oldest sisters were stepsisters. My dad married a lady who had been married before. She had two daughters, Doris and Rosie Lee. She and Dad had two daughters, Alice and Albertha. Then they separated and she went back to her first husband and had four more children.

Dad married Gussie, my mother, and they had me. Sometimes Alice and Albertha would come to stay with us during the school year and go back to Mississippi for the summer. Doris and Rosie Lee moved to Chicago when they married. Rosie had one daughter, and Doris had one son. Those were my sisters because they were my sister's sister. They were good to me and it made no difference. In those days I guess that's the way southerners were. When Doris' first marriage broke up, I was sorry because I really liked her husband. She went back south for awhile and met a man that would impact my life. They moved to our house in Chicago Heights at 1421 Lowe Avenue. Doris and James had one son and daughter. She was pregnant. James was a gentle, caring man who loved the Lord. He went to church with us when we went to Reverend Stevenson's and visited with me when I went to Portland Street. James was Baptist born and Baptist bred and when he died he'd be Baptist dead. He messed with my newfound theology. He didn't smoke or drink. He was kind. He didn't curse, wasn't flirty, and was a good family man, but he wasn't Pentecostal. So, was he really saved? Was this good man who had accepted Jesus Christ as his personal savior going to hell?

I was too young to have those answers. I should have been too young to have those questions. Was I taught that my church was the only church? Was I taught that we were better than others were, or was that just my interpretation of what was being taught?

James and Doris, with their four kids (two were born while living with us), moved to the west side of Chicago where he got killed going into his building coming from a Deacon's meeting at his Baptist church. The story goes that gangs were gunning for his oldest son.

Some days when I was working on the West Side, if the weather was too bad for me to take the IC home, I'd call them and spend the night with them. She was my sister. Doris was the one who kept me from hitting Aunt Leatha with that iron skillet. Doris looked like me. (I wonder).

Rosie lived on the south side. She was a glamour puss. I thought she was beautiful. She was a cross between Leslie Uggams and Diane Carroll. When I was on the south side of Chicago, I would stop by Rosie's house.

I never got a chance to meet their mother, Doll, because she was down south until I moved to Minnesota. But her children were my family. The daughter next to me, Dorothy Mae spent a few nights with me. They called my dad Daddy Murphy. He treated them all like his children.

After my mom, there was my brother James. He lived with us for about ten years. He was my only brother. I didn't know he liked me until one night I got him a date with my girlfriend's sister. He, at eighteen, had gotten a car and my friend wanted to go to the naval base, which was about two hours away from us, to see her brother. James agreed. The four of us went and had fun. He was so happy when he let the girls off at their house. He asked me if I wanted to drive home. I said yes. I did really well. I pulled into the alley to turn around to park in front of our house. James said, "I'd better do that". I didn't have the car in park so when he got out to go around, his foot touched mine, which was over the accelerator, and backed the car into a parked car. He jumped in the car and pulled it over. A man came out in long white underwear and a shotgun and said, "Stop, or I'll shoot"! We stopped. He called the police; he was a policeman.

James made me promise that I wouldn't tell that I was driving. He also made me promise not to tell where he was when they took him to jail. James told me I would be the laughing stock of Bloom Township High School, where I was a junior, if they knew I was driving that car. My brother really liked me! He was protecting me.

It was about three o'clock in the morning. Dad and James worked the 7 a.m. to 3 p.m. shift at Victor Chemical. Dad went into wake James up and, to his surprise . . . no James. He came to my mom and demanded to know where James was. I was in a dilemma. I had promised James I wouldn't tell and my father was demanding I tell. I asked him to ask the neighbors. I went to school, but worried all day about James. When I got home, Dad and Miss Mary had gotten James out of jail. He hadn't registered for the Army, so, instead of prosecuting him, he was sent to the Army in 1952. He stayed about six months and was in the reserves for a few years. He paid for the repair of the cars.

Daddy and Miss Mary didn't ask me what happened. They took James' word, I told my dad after I left Grandpa Alex in 1973. He told me he knew it. Do you think Reverend Stevenson told him? She gave readings.

When I was twenty, I moved back home from Aunt Flo's. Daddy, Miss Mary, and James were living in the house on Fifth Avenue, Aunt Mattie Early's house. I was lonely for my family. I worked the summer at Spiegel.

but was often late. Spiegel wasn't having it. They said one more late start, don't bother coming in. I was taking several buses from the suburbs to get to 35<sup>th</sup> Street in Chicago. I took the earliest bus, but it didn't work for me. I'm not a bell person. They had bells for when you were to be in your seat, and when you went to lunch, etc. Well, I didn't go back, but I called my union steward and told him I was available. I had left my other job, in good standing, so he got me a job in a small store on 16<sup>th</sup> and Drake on the West Side of Chicago.

I went home to Chicago Heights every night. Well, I was there mostly alone. Miss Mary had told me, when I was in school, that when I left Daddy, she was leaving also. I don't know what happened, but Daddy was spending nights away from home. He had started taking alcohol for medicinal purposes; wine for his blood, beer to flush his kidneys, whiskey for his cold, and gin to make him sleep.

I thought there was no sense in me commuting five hours a day to an empty house, so I moved two blocks from my job. One night after James left, Daddy took up with a young lady. Who knows when this relationship started? Queenie had five children. One night, the Welfare Department sent a spy to knock on the door. Murphy opened up the door in his sleeping clothes. Well, they told him if he married Queenie they would let the five kids stay on welfare, and he'd just take care of his wife. They married and she never saw another check. So I'm told. Daddy had a good job and he was a hustler, so it really didn't matter much.

Queenie is about ten years older than I am. When I got married, she and I had children together. She had her kids at home because she was afraid to be strapped down in the hospital delivery room. I have nine more siblings from Queenie. She brought five to the marriage; Bessie and Dessie (twins), Calvin, Geraldine and Mattie. Then with Murphy . . . Christine, Murphy Jr., Michael and Michelle (twins). So, it was hard explaining all these variables in my family . . ."This is my sister's aunt or grandmother. This is my uncle on my brother's side". I was determined not to put my kids through that. I wanted all of them to be by one man. I did not go into marriage looking out. I was in it for keeps.

# CHAPTER EIGHT

I was careful in selecting a mate. When I saw something I definitely couldn't, nor wouldn't, live with, I left the person alone. I knew I was a unique person, so I would need a special person to hold my interest. I fell in love with Grandpa Alex when I was fourteen.

One night we were in revival at our church. Elder Samuel Allen was preaching. In walked two real handsome men. Their hair was conked and pompadored; one light-skinned and the other a little browner. Elder Allen told them and others that they were on their way to hell. He preached a good long sermon that night. Well, the next night they came back and got saved. Both of their mothers' were saved.

Many young people got saved in this meeting. I brought several. My friends had to get saved or we couldn't be friends anymore. We would have nothing in common. My cousin, J. W., got saved, so that was another person in our house to torment Daddy.

One night after Alex had been saved, about a month, he walked Miss Mary and me home. He grabbed my hand in his huge hands and we talked. Miss Mary was walking and talking with friends ahead of us. Alex told me that night that God told him that I was his wife. I was fourteen (1950) and he was twenty. Well, I was a little snippet and responded, "Well, He hasn't told me anything yet!

But I was in love. We talked on the phone. We sat together when the church went to places on a chartered bus. We saw each other three times a week at church. Then he slacked off church, come summer. His buddy still came. Well, I couldn't see him. My dad was still strict. So, if Alex wasn't at church, there was no place I could see him. Then I was spending summers in Chicago with my mother and Willie. I had a hard time trying to find a name for him, Mr. Willie.

It wasn't too hard for me missing Alex because I enjoyed life with my mother and Willie. We went fishing and he was reinstated in a church. He was an awesome teacher. He made me want to learn. He made Sunday school interesting.

When I went back in early September, I'd take up where I left off with my church, family, friends and Alex, if he was at the church. He had a problem. During summers his fancy would turn to the "world". So, we would quit every time he left church. I don't think people were encouraged to come when they were not walking circumspectly. I contend that hearing the Word and being around positive people will give a person an incentive to do better.

Well, Alex went into the Army and was finally sent to Korea. We wrote each other but I wasn't convinced he was the right one. So I talked with other guys. When Alex came home on furlough, a girl got pregnant. Of course, my dad forbade me to talk with him. He threatened to shoot us if he saw us talking on the street. My heart was broken, but I snapped back because, evidently, he wasn't my husband. Michael was born April 28, 1952. I was sixteen years old. I thought they were going to marry. I didn't want it said that I was the cause of them not marrying. My dad said, "If he did it to her, he'd do it to you". Daddy hated Alex and the feeling was mutual.

I went to Chicago every other weekend, but I can't remember a boyfriend over there. My step-dad was just as strict as Dad, but we also did so much I didn't have time to mind. My girlfriend (one year younger than I) and I went to Curtis Candy Company one summer and she got a job by lying about her age. But I didn't get it because I wouldn't lie and their age requirement was 16.

Well, after eight years of on again, off again, romance, Alex and I were married on December 5, 1958. I had not seen him for two years until six weeks before we got married. One night Alex called me and said he wasn't coming to church because he was sick. On the way home from church, a girlfriend and I decided to drop by and see the sick person. I never went to his house, but thought it was safe with another person; and I was visiting the sick. I knocked, then identified myself. A little shuffling and he finally came to the door, There was a lady sitting on the side of the bed (not Michael's mom), and a bottle of Vodka was on the night stand. We talked a little and Marie and I left,

When I got about four blocks away, I got so angry that I told Marie to go on. I was going back. I went back and pounded on that door like a policeman. He came out dressed and walked me down the street. I was telling him what I thought about this shady action. He laughed at me. He said, "Are you serious"? I hit, kicked and bit him. He put his arms around me so that the people wouldn't know I was fighting him. The next day I moved to Chicago to live with a couple (Aunt Flo's friend) and their child. It was beneath me to fight on the street. I was saved and dignified—oh I had to go! In those two years, I was engaged twice. I was engaged once while staying at Aunt Fto's house.

Strange things always happened to end those engagements; things I couldn't live with. I wanted a saved man. Aunt Flo let me know you could be saved in other churches. So, this man came into the store where I worked. He was tall, dark, handsome, and had a good job. My family loved him. He was originally from Memphis. He was a church guy. He sang in a quartet.

He was too good to be true. He was twenty-three and had never been married and had never lived with anyone. He was also willing to buy a "pig in a poke". He didn't pressure me for sex. He respected my wishes. He could really turn me on, but I was determined I wasn't having sex before marriage. But I didn't want to marry anyone who couldn't make me want to.

My heart has never ruled my head. I prayed about this too-good-to-be-true man. I had no doubt that he loved me. I still believe that he did. He waited for me for five years after I married Alex. One day it came to me to fast for three days and nights. I did and prayed sincerely to see if this was the one for me. He had furnished an apartment for us and everyone was happy, waiting for the wedding. Even my dad loved him.

He went away to Army Reserves and his car disappeared. He had left it in our yard. I called camp and they had him return my call. He said he would take care of it. On the second day of the fast, a lady called Aunt Flo's house. My mother answered the phone. (My mother, thirty-nine years old, was staying at Aunt Flo's house to recuperate from a tubal pregnancy operation). She said, "Tell Ruby to be careful where she and Neil go tonight". I continued the fast. On the third day she called again and told Mother she was his ex-wife. After many lies and stand-offs, I found out (maybe) that he married a woman who had been married before. She was older than he was. He went to the Army and she went back to her husband. He got his divorce on whatever legal procedure he had to and he thought he could hide the fact from me. I could never marry someone who had been married before so I broke it off. He came by every three months to see if I had changed my mind.

You would have been different people had I married him. Would we be in Minnesota? Would I have been a pastor's wife? Would I have chosen your names? God is awesome! I have forty-one beautiful people in my life that I wouldn't have met had my life taken another turn. Then, I was engaged to the preacher who would have married me to hide his gay tendencies. It was so special how I found this out. Prayer works. And, God won't let you get into a mess if you trust Him.

He was a good preacher, singer and musician. I wanted a saved man. Alex couldn't keep it together, so this man chose me and I agreed. We were to get married at 5 a.m. on Easter Sunday morning in 1959, with top hats, canes and capes for the men. I can't remember what the ladies were wearing. He was doing all the planning. He was in Boston and the wedding was to be there. We argued by letter and phone about where the wedding was to take place. I told him the wedding should be in the lady's hometown. He said to save money. It would be cheaper for me to fly there than for him to fly to me and both of us to fly back. "Well, if you discard that entire getup we could save more money" was my argument.

During our dialogue, we discussed sex; which he had planned three nights a week. Not on Sunday because we'd be tired from church, Monday, Wednesday and Saturday were the three set days! You see we'd go to church on Tuesdays and Fridays. I was inexperienced, but I am a spontaneous person. Planning didn't sound romantic to me.

When he told me we would eat with full place settings and candlelight every night, I was through! If I was working, going to school, or having babies, I couldn't see how I could do all of that. I was overwhelmed before I got into ft.

He grew up in my church and had gone to Boston to go to school. The Easter weekend in 1958, we had spent the night with a married couple in Chicago. He slept with the man and I slept with the lady. She was up most of the night cooking. We ate and took the "L" down to the Loop. I overheard them talking about seeing how many men they could excite on the train. I stored that in my memory bank. The man who was a great musician in the church denomination where I belonged, was rumored to be homosexual, but he was married and saved, so I didn't believe the rumor.

I couldn't marry him with these doubts; Let everyone be fully persuaded in his own heart, just don't involve me. Don't mess up my life. People were in the closets then, but I didn't want anyone hiding behind me. I can compete with another woman, but I can't compete with a man.

My second fiancée never married. His mother blamed me. He pastored a church. I would call him several times a year. He would be surprised every time I called him. Then I lost track. I didn't dislike him, but I couldn't let my life be altered without my consent. If I had chosen that life It would be different, but that wasn't what I wanted out of life. If I saw it coming and went in head-on, it would be my fault.

Then there was the doctor. You see, I was almost twenty-two and I was determined I wasn't going to spend another winter sleeping with an iron to keep my feet warm (we had radiators). My doctor had spent five years in Germany, going to school while in the Army. He was born and raised in our denomination. He asked me for oral sex. That scared me. I started avoiding him. When he finally caught up with me, I told him what scared me. He said it wasn't a requirement. Well, I was through with him. You young folks might do a lot of stuff. That's why I gave up so much kissing. I might kiss you on the cheek, but I don't know where your mouth has been and I don't want to be a second-hand anything.

One of my bosses asked me to cheat the customer for him. On a cash register you could add a certain amount at the beginning of the receipt and pull that part out. The rest will be on the ticket. But the amount that was added will be computed in your total. So, if a big order comes through, the manager might give you a code to add. Anyway, I told the manager that if I had no conscience to steal from the customer for him, I wouldn't have a conscience to steal from him for me. If I was going to hell, I told him, I was going for me.

People at my church asked me why did I stay at that job. I told them I stayed because the one thousand people who came through my register got a fair price. If I left, they might find someone who would cheat and all the registers would be cheating. When they wanted to promote someone to collect the money and count it, I was the one chosen. It wasn't the girls who were cheating for him. That's the place I was working when I got pregnant with Barton. We got robbed at gun point and Bart jumped in

45

my stomach. Do you think that had something to with his fascination for guns?

Anyway, after the last engagement episode, I remember that Alex said, "When you're serious about getting married, get in touch". I hadn't seen him for two years so I wrote him a letter addressed to his sister Pauline. I just said, "When you get this letter, please call me" and included my phone number. In about a week she saw him and told him about my letter waiting tor him. He called me in about ten days from the mailing of the letter. I asked him to meet me on 63$^{rd}$ and Halsted in Chicago. He did. In six weeks we were married. I knew Alex. I knew he had never been married, I knew his problem was sex. That was why he couldn't walk in victory very long. I knew he was a good looking, street-wise, country boy. So we married on December 5, 1958. In the years we have been married, he has never hit me or cursed me.

# CHAPTER NINE

Alex and I are still opposites even after thirty-nine years of marriage. He grew up very poor, so he says. He was born January 7, 1930. I didn't think the depression would have been bad in the South. He was born in Hopkinsville, Kentucky. I would have thought you could grow your food there. I use to write to his sister, Birdie, at 1000 Younglove Street. When I went down to his Aunt Lettie Bell's funeral, I saw that Hopkinsville was a city. Unlike the South, I had experienced in Cleveland, Mississippi, we were five miles from the town. In Hopkinsville they had stores, bars, and clubs right in town.

I had a lot of friends. When I was in high school, there were seven of us girls who hung together. They were all from my church. Even after school we remained friends. I liked a bunch of people around. Alex was mostly a loner. I liked people at my house while Alex went out to be with people. I liked to stay up at night to do my cleaning (Aunt Leatha taught me that). Alex wanted me in bed at night. I wanted to go to church at least every Sunday. He wasn't ready for church yet. I worked on jobs till I was tired of them (usually I was bored in a year or so). Alex usually got jobs where he was laid off part of the year. He was street-wise and I couldn't even use slang. I couldn't listen to Blues or Jazz while Jazz was his favorite music.

Six weeks after we got married, I found out he liked to drink and spend every *Friday* night out . . . all night. He liked to reward himself for working all week. I panicked! I thought he was dead. I called every jail in the city and surrounding towns, every hospital and even the last jailer made me feel like a fool; this was normal behavior for many men. Every time a car stopped outside, I would jump up and look out of the window; being very disappointed when it wasn't him. I'd do this all night long and finally, hearing his footsteps on the stairs, I'd fall asleep from exhaustion. When he came in, I was sleeping like a baby. So it became a pattern for him to celebrate every Friday night. I never asked him where he had been because I hate anyone lying to me. I felt if he was somewhere he could tell me about, he would. So, by not saying anything, I taught him that it was okay with me if he spent every Friday night out.

One Friday, I decided I would teach him a lesson. I went over to one of my friend's house and, after talking, fell asleep. I woke up about 2 a.m., called a cab, and went home. When I got out of the cab, I slammed the door and said goodbye to the male cab driver; hoping Alex would hear him reply. When I got upstairs, my nerves failed so I tipped in the bathroom and changed my clothes. I tipped to the bedroom so I wouldn't wake him up. To my surprise, he wasn't even there. So, that was the end of my tit-for-tat. I stayed home and silently seethed for years. After Barton was born, I could sleep while Alex was out. I would put him in the bed with me. I gained fifty pounds with Barton. I was in labor for three days in the hospital. In those days, it was rumored that if it was a choice between saving the mother or the child, the mother would be sacrificed. She had had her chance at life, so it was the child's turn now.

I had never experienced this much pain in my life. I don't want to discourage you, my granddaughters, from having babies. If it were so horrific, population would be at an all-time low. There would be no repeaters.

With Barton jumping in my stomach in the robbery, the commute being too much for me, and my grandfather dying when I was five months pregnant, I quit work. In my first trimester, I could eat no meat, eggs, or coffee. I could eat mostly fruits and some vegetables if they weren't greasy. Being at home and mostly inactive triggered my weight gain. These are some reasons labor is laborious. I was in the hospital five days after Barton was born . . . in the hospital eight days altogether.

Alex broke his leg the day I came home from the hospital. We had no insurance. I was unable to work and any little savings were gone for the hospital bills. I had stitches from a to z. I had not adjusted to a normal sex life. Sex was uncomfortable even after two years of marriage. Do you think that's why Alex went out?

On our honeymoon, I thought, "Is this what people are losing their souls over? Well, Alex said he had a talk with the doctor and asked him to leave a couple of stitches open. I made him wait the entire six weeks.

Sex became pleasant. I'll have to write an expose' under an assumed name because I can't tell my grand kids everything! Anyway, I didn't lose weight after Barton. I was nursing and not exercising. In five months I was pregnant again. We thought nursing was a birth control. Gotcha!

Poppa's funeral (my grandfather) was sad and funny. I was the most pleasant person when I was pregnant. Things that were suppose to make me angry actually made me laugh. I had heard that women got their husbands up in the middle of the night to send them out looking for strawberries in the wintertime. I knew a place in Chicago's Loop that sold out-of-season fruit. I'd go to bed with the intentions of waking up craving some and sending Alex to find it. Well, I would sleep all night long.

Poppa's funeral was at Payne Chapel AME Church on Center Avenue, We would go to his church every Father's Day. Poppa was Methodist, but he always marred Baptist women. All four of his wives were Baptist. We were raised Baptist. The Methodist Church was the intellectual church in the Black community. They sang hymns and anthems from books. I never saw anyone shout there. Well, his fourth wife screamed so loud at the funeral I'm sure Poppa was even embarrassed. She said in C over high C, "Oh, I won't have anybody to play with anymore"! I couldn't contain myself. I whooped! My laughter made my whole body tremble. Alex held me the way he did when I beat him up on the street; he sheltered me in his big arms and people thought I was crying.

The first month pregnant with Barry, I was sad and I had a drunken husband. He drank on Fridays. I had a five-month old baby and was pregnant again. I only gained twenty-nine pounds with Barry and lost twenty-seven pounds at his birth. I hadn't lost Barton's weight yet. I loved to read. Alex had only read one book when we got married. He had a great personality. He was spoiled when I got him. Aunt Sis, his oldest sister, raised him. She picked the bones out of his fish for him. Well, I bought whiting and boneless perch. But, I did fix his plate and brought it to him.

One day he said, "Is there any ice in the refrigerator"? I got up and got him some ice. He didn't ask me to, but I interpreted his question to be a request. I have been locked into what I heard him say for thirty-nine years. One day I ironed his pants and tried as I may, I couldn't get the crease sharp on that permanent crease. He had square knees. In my day the wife was expected to do the ironing, cooking, cleaning, and washing. When he found cat paws in his shirts, he heard me say, "I don't know how to iron men's clothes". Daddy always had a wife to iron his things. I was only responsible for washing and ironing my own clothes. Alex taught all of his sons to do their own clothes. "Mama will have you going around looking tacky". One day I washed his wool sweater and shrunk it to a child's size. He heard me say I didn't know how to wash men's clothes either. So, he washes his own clothes too.

Alex and I went bowling every Saturday night with two more couples who were a part of the DuKays (night owl, single). We had found some friends in common and something we could both enjoy doing. We did it for about six months, till I got pregnant with Barton. I didn't want to risk a miscarriage so I gave up bowling. Alex used to win dance contests. He was a social butterfly. I was locked into my values of not going to "worldly" places.

Alex made me promise when we got married, never to make him a bologna sandwich. Evidently a lady he use to date starved him. I worked at a grocery store and I got a discount on food. I fixed him five pork chops or hamburgers, or other creative things, a dessert, a fruit, and a love letter. I had three uncles who worked where Alex finally settled down to work. My mother's brother, Rufus Perkins, Aunt Della's (who died in childbirth) husband, Burnett Hughes, Sr., (Uncle Toad), and Mother's sister, Aunt Mattie's husband, John Whitlock (Uncle Jr.), were Alex's drinking buddies. He was closer to Uncle Toad. Somehow, one of them mentioned my steamy letters to me. The nerve of Alex sharing my love letters with other men and my uncles in particular. I quit writing!

I used to boil Barton's diapers and bottles to sterilize them. Alex would get on his knees over the bathtub and wash diapers. This macho man had no problem doing this. He was a perfect gentleman. We walked on the outside and wanted me to hold his arm when we walked. I had to learn to let him lead the way as we walked. I didn't dance, so I knew nothing about leading and following. There were two doors. Why couldn't I decide which one to go in? If we had to go between cars, why should he decide whether we went on the right side or the left side? You see, since Dad raised me, I had masculine thoughts, and since Grandpa Alex's sister raised him, and with all of his he-man looks, he had a feminine quality.

I would buy the things I needed and wanted for the house, but I was only taught to keep it clean, not make 'a pretty'. Alex knew how to make it pretty, not keep it clean. So, we made a great pair. I'd buy and he'd put it in place.

# CHAPTER TEN

I was so thrilled when the doctor told me I was pregnant. It was a miracle. He and another doctor told me I couldn't get pregnant. He was amazed, and almost angry. He was the best doctor in town; at least the most popular. He said, "I don't know how you got pregnant, but you won't be able to deliver this baby because you have a male-like pelvis and it won't open. You will have to have a cesarean". I told him I believed in the power of prayer. In the three days of labor, it never occurred to me to have a C-section. After Barton was born the doctor woke me up and said, "If you have another baby, you must promise me you won't gain but twenty pounds or I won't be responsible for your life".

He had been my doctor since the Black Dex and I really loved him. But, I couldn't go back to someone who talked like that. He wasn't mean, just factual. We had a great history. I would sit and ask him many questions. He told me I was trying to learn in a half-hour what took him sixteen years to learn.

Barton was the prettiest baby I had ever seen. He was born with male pattern baldness with straight hair in the back. We brushed it to the front. The doctor said he was a hungry baby so we started him on a little cereal at five days old. I opened the nipple a touch. Plus, I nursed him. When they brought him to my bed, he was sucking his two fingers (ring and middle) on his left hand.

He started sleeping all night at six weeks. He was a schedule baby. I could feed him, clean him up, burp him, and play with him for a few minutes and he would go back to sleep for about three hours. He was the best baby. "If it doesn't come out in the wash, it will come out in the rinse", was a family joke.

Barton got his first two teeth the day he was six months old. I made his baby food. I cooked carrots, beets, squash, etc., for him. I was a proud and thankful mother. Alex baby-sat and rocked him. He loved to be across our lap and patted firmly on his back. When we would quit, he'd squirm. On Friday nights, he'd become my sleeping buddy. I was never awake again waiting for Alex. I had my son.

Barton resented being replaced as baby in fourteen months. He hadn't finished being number one. He started walking at fifteen months. He was born two weeks after JFK, Jr. so I measured his progress with the President's son. I knew JFK, Jr. was getting all the nutrition he needed so I didn't panic at Barton not walking at nine months like I did.

Barton was a manipulator. He hoodwinked Barry out of his good milk, often. When the bottle had been in the bed all night, he offered it to Barry and said, "You see if it sour. If I had just fixed Barry a fresh bottle, Barton would say, "Yet me see if it sour"! He could always talk anything out of Barry.

He used to run from fights. His dad sent him back out one day and he won the fight. His teachers said they were glad when he began taking up for himself. His principal said he never started a fight, but he always finished it.

One day in junior high a boy picked on his cousin Sandy. Maybe the boy spit on her. Barton protected her ferociously. All the other kids had to say was, "I'm Barton's sister, or brother, or cousin", and no one bothered them. Somewhere during the junior high years, he got a chip on his shoulder. He couldn't act it out at home so he did it in school.

When Barton was in high school, Alex had gotten saved and was very strict. He didn't allow Barton to participate in sports for various reasons. I had to fast every day until after school to get Barton through the day without incidents. We found out that even though we sent him to school every day, he was missing classes. Finally the music teacher fessed up to letting Barton be in his class all day. He could play drums, guitar, horns, keyboards, etc. He would fit in wherever needed. He said Barton wasn't going to class, so he chose the lesser of the two evils. Evil is evil!

Somewhere during this time, two girls got pregnant, one White, one Black. Can't imagine where he met the White girl, she was from Anoka, a suburb of Minneapolis. One day he and the Black girl got in a fight and she called the police on him . . . rightly so. We didn't know about either of the pregnancies. He quit the Black girl and denied that the baby was his probably because she did call the police. It was many years before I knew Sherise was ours. She looked so much like her half-white sister Lorie. One was jet black, the other golden; both beautiful! When Landon was born, Barton married Carolyn (the White girl). Her father was a pastor also. By this time, Alex had chosen the straight and narrow and had started pastoring a church. So, I think Barton thought he and Carolyn had more in common. They had five children, Landon, Lone, Liston, L'Nae, and La Mondre. The rest of Barton's children are Sherise (mother Christine), Ronnie (mother Charon), Stephen, Tonya and Tar'race (mother Kris), and Rhubie and Bartonna (mother Paula) . . . twelve children in all.

Barton was diagnosed with diabetes and high blood pressure. It was an adult on-set so it could be controlled with diet and exercise. If he loses weight, he can avoid complications. Children beware! I was also diagnosed the same. I control mine with garlic, being eighty-five percent vegetarian, and with exercise. Grandma Gussie died from diabetes complications . . . kidney failure.

One day we went to visit a city where our friends lived. We stayed in a motel for three days then we spent the night with them. She cooked the best sausage, shrimp and chicken over rice. The next morning I took a shower. Well, I have a fear of falling in the shower. So as soon as I turned off the water I stepped out. I put down towels when I'm at home. I didn't see anything hut the rug to step on so I did. The rug was wet and the husband made a real big deal about the damp rug. That made me decide not to stay with anyone else. If I couldn't afford a motel or hotel, I'd stay home. Everyone has his or her peculiar ways. Mine is that I use plenty of towels because I bathe at least once a day, but I don't linger after it's over. I can stay in a bath for almost an hour, but when I decide to stand up, I must get out.

I contend you can get along with anyone as long as you don't violate his or her rules. But you have to know what those rules are. I do not take a vacation at someone else's house. I cannot lie up in bed while someone else is working. I can't expect them to wait on me and I don't want to get up and cook and clean while on vacation. I could have stayed at home to do that.

# CHAPTER ELEVEN

Barry was born February 11, 1962. After the doctor told me he wouldn't be responsible for my life, I wrote to the University of Illinois Research Hospital and told them about my diagnosis; my difficult labor, Barton's size (nine pounds), and me being pregnant so soon afterward. They quickly responded and I was admitted to the clinic. I commuted again to the West Side of Chicago. My friend's daughter, Linda, was my sidekick. We made a day of it, once a month. A family member cared for Barton. After we left the hospital, we would go to Walgreen's on Randolph and State for a good cafeteria meal.

We were moving the night I started labor. I was at Daddy and Queenie's house. Daddy called his former choice for my husband to drive us to the hospital. He (I'll call him Paul) drove Mother, Daddy, Queenie and me to the hospital. Alex was moving and couldn't go. They left me there after a few hours, after they knew for sure that I was in true labor and that they would keep me. The doctors assured them I would be okay. I felt so alone. Other women had their husbands there. In 1962 only your mother or your husband could be in the labor room. Since I had two mothers there, I wonder it they would have let both of them stay.

Because this was a teaching institution, I had plenty of company—students and interns who had to learn Gynecology and O.B. I was in labor for about fifteen hours. A lot belier than three days! I had two male interns at my bedside at all times, messaging my back when I had a labor pain. I had the best care possible. They seemed to really care. The lady in the next bed had her husband and must have had natural childbirth classes. She talked to her husband calmly when she was in pain. I was very emotional and didn't have to tell anyone when my pains were.

Everyone on the floor was privy to my pain. The bed next to me kept emptying and I was still there.

Finally it was time. They rushed me to the delivery room. My water broke and I saw the surprise on the doctor's faces. I don't think they had delivered many babies. Then Barry came, ten pounds, eight and a half ounces. They were amazed. When the afterbirth came, they weighed it at three and a half pounds. We estimated that I had lost almost fourteen pounds of water, because I lost twenty-seven pounds at the birth. I had wondered how I could love another baby because I loved Barton so much. Barry had a head full of curly hair. He looked like a cuddly little Indian baby—very pretty.

Their policy at the hospital was to bring "mom" the baby after twenty-four hours. When they brought Barry to me he wouldn't eat, but was sucking the ring and middle fingers. After examination they told me he had Hirschsprung Disease. A nerve was missing in his bowels, which made it impossible for him to push his bowels through. They wanted to operate and give him a colostomy.

I was there alone, so I called my Prayerband leader for advice. He said, "When you're praying for your mate to be saved, you don't know what methods God will use". My thoughts then and now is punish a person for their own sins. Don't punish my child. I don't believe that was God's doing.

They let me go home and they operated on Barry when he was two days old. I agonized. I wondered what did I do to cause this. This was the year of the Thalidomide scandal. Many children were born deformed in 1962. I was given morning sickness medicine, but I only took several because I have an aversion to medicine ever since the Black Dex. I just eliminated things that made me nauseous. Did I take this dangerous drug? I don't know what was in those morning sickness pills. Was it because I sprayed my kitchen for bugs? Was it because on my first visit to the hospital they used a giant spray gun and stood afar to spray your genital areas? I guess they saw so many people . . . some that were not clean . . . that they protected themselves from lice or venereal diseases. Maybe all or none of these things contributed to his illness.

When they taught me how to care for Barry, I was overwhelmed. I had to use tissue around his stoma. There were two outside of his stomach. I had to put enough to catch the entire stool. I had a diaper around his back, one on his bottom, and two across his stomach to catch the stool. I used pins to fasten the diaper around his waist. I was told to change this every four hours or when I knew he needed changing. We invested in a crib diaper service.

Here I was with a husband who was not saved, and two babies. Both babies were on bottles, neither one walking, and one was sick. How I ached for my little baby and me. I think Alex couldn't believe that something less than perfect came from him. He drank more. I became very protective of my baby. My family wondered why I didn't leave the baby with them. I knew how hard it was for me to keep him clean, and I didn't want anyone feeling sorry for my baby. He was my responsibility. Sometimes people would come and visit me and ask what they could do. I said just watch the kids while I take a nap. I was there, so if my kids needed me, or if Barry had a bowel movement, they could wake me up.

When I had to run out to the store, Mother Phillips (who lived downstairs) would come up for the minutes I needed. There were times, because his skin was so sensitive, that he would get a severe rash around his stoma. We used all the diaper rash solutions that were available. Sometimes I would lay him on a blanket and sheet, naked, and let a fan blow on his rash. I kept him as clean and dry as possible. He had several baths a day. His skin was too sensitive for the plastic bags.

When I really began asking God "Why us?" it would be time for our visit to the University Hospital. When I would get there I would see babies born with no ears, or born with their bladder on the outside of their body, ones with no feet, or Down Syndrome babies, etc. When I left that hospital, I'd put my baby under my arm and almost skip out, thanking God that Barry was as well off as he was.

It was time for Barry to have surgery again. They were going to correct his condition. He was eleven months old. Alex and I sat during those agonizing hours of surgery. I'm praying, "Lord, don't take my baby". The doctor's came out grim-faced and told me they had to give him an iliostomy, which was worse than a colostomy, the bowels were more liquefied.

Sister Lang and I went on a three-day shut in at our church. Every time I woke up, she was praying. Alex and Mother kept Barton and Barry. On the second day of our fast, our pastor's wife came in to tell us that we had a miracle. Barry's stoma had disappeared and there was bowel movement coming from his rectum in his bottom diaper.

We finished our three days and I made plans to take Barry to the hospital. They laughed at me when I told them that there was bowel movement in his bottom diaper. He lay there on the table and had two bowel movements right in front of them. They had severed the connection there was no way he could be having a bowel movement from his rectum. After the frenzy, they kept Barry for six weeks. They couldn't explain it. When he came back home his stoma was extended. We had thought they could operate and connect his bowels since the nerve was working right. It had been the longest he had ever stayed in the hospital at one time.

I contacted Children's Memorial Hospital and they accepted Barry in their clinic. The doctor who perfected the pull-through surgery was Barry's doctor. In the pull-through, they would pull the damaged bowel through till the healthy bowel could push the bowel through. Well, we went through surgery again in anguish . . . heart in my mouth, praying all the time, and wiping tears. Finally the doctor came out and they had given him another colostomy. So now he had had one iliostomy and two colostomy operations. I was so disappointed.

When it was time for him to go to school, the principal in our hometown said he wouldn't be responsible for a handicapped child. He could go to a school with the mentally handicapped, or we could move to Chicago. We had friends in Minneapolis, Mattie (who was my best friend), and Lawrence (who was Alex's best friend). I called them and she told me about the Michael Dowling School. I called them and they accepted us over the phone. We made arrangements to move from Illinois to Minnesota.

On October 23, 1967, Alex and several of his friends moved us here. We had sent Mattie the money and she had rented a house for us. We put the furniture in the house, but the gas and lights weren't on. So we had to spend a week or so with Mattie and Lawrence. Alex and his friends went back to Illinois. He was to work until January, but he quit in early December and came to us. Mother quit her job right afterwards and came also.

We lived across the street from Harrison School, but we were in the John Hay school district. I had to get a referral from our district for Barry to go to the Michael Dowling School. Mrs. Rhinehart, the school's social worker, suggested we try Barry at Harrison School, and if he had an accident, he could come right home—just across the street. In January Barry started school. Mattie's mother baby-sat for me.

Barry was adjusting well, so in March I started work at TCOIC. Mrs. Rhinehart sent me a public health nurse. Elaine Zech was a lifesaver. She came to OIC to find out how we were adjusting. She visited the house to see Barry. She suggested we go to General Hospital for his medical care. They scheduled surgery for summer break. I worked the day of his surgery. I had been through this many times. I told the Lord that I was selfish in asking Him not to take my baby. I put Barry totally in God's hands. I wasn't the one who had to be humiliated when his bowels moved involuntarily and whom the kids laughed at when he was stinking. Probably the reason Barry is a loner today is because kids and people can be so cruel.

One day, when Barry was about four, I came into the room and he was trying to change himself. He made a mess, but I knew he was trying to help and he didn't want that stuff on him. Sometimes we would be going out the door and he would be soiled from neck to knees. When I would clean him, many times he would look up at me with those beautiful, large brown eyes and say, "Thank you Mommy". My heart would break. I cried for my son.

That evening, I went to the hospital and saw that Barry had made it through the surgery. When the doctor talked to me, I didn't want to hear small talk; cut to the chase. Does he have another colostomy? He looked at me like I was crazy. Barry was put back together and they were waiting on a bowel movement.

In about a week Barry was well and he came home. We had to teach him how to use the pot at six years old. He went back to the hospital twice with a distended stomach from all the adhesions due to the four major surgeries. He survived and is the healthiest of all the children. When he was little, he was diagnosed with Thallasemia Minor, a Mediterranean blood disease (the opposite of Leukemia). Our family has a tendency toward anemia.

Whenever I would leave the hospital, Barry would scream and perform. I would feel so guilty leaving, but visiting hours would be over. I had to go. The nurse told me to go to the elevator, let it close, and tip back to his room in one minute. I did. He screamed till the elevator closed. I went back to his room and saw him playing with his roommates. So, I left feeling better.

Barry had to repeat Kindergarten because he only had half a year. The only other time he was sick was when he had the flu, pneumonia, and bronchitis for about six weeks. He was in high school. He got hooked on "All My Children" during this time and asked me to watch it for him when he started back to school.

We have a special bond, but because he's a middle child he thinks he's overlooked. Michael is Alex's first born, Barton is mine; Bretta is the only girl; and Byron is both of our babies. Barry has a thirst for knowledge, like me. Barry's children are Duran (mother Paula), Barry Jr., Maleka, and Alex (by his wife Mary).

At fifteen Barry shared his first sexual experience with me. I was appalled. He was astonished that I didn't want to share his joy of such a glorious experience. I encouraged my children to talk with me, but I wasn't ready for that. His girl got pregnant with that few minutes of joy.

# CHAPTER TWELVE

July 14, 1983, was the day we buried Great Grandma Gussie. She was born November 11, 1916. She thought she was born in 1915. She married Murphy in 1934. They had a little girl named Ernestine, but she died from Diphtheria. I was born June 16, 1936. Gussie and Murphy's relationship was turbulent, to put it mildly. She was a version of Lena Horne with a flatter nose and a shade lighter. Murphy was a B. B. King. I could only hear snatches of their courtship and marriage. Our people were very secretive about who's who and what's what. I do know that grandparents did raise their grandchildren as they own never divulging that secret. I know that polygamy was practiced. I know that bigamy was also a way of life. You left one and married another. Not quite like jumping the broom, just by general knowledge and consent. I don't know how the church accepted this practice, other than culture might have superseded written word. Could it be also that many slaves, including the preacher, couldn't read? So, I don't know if my mother was married before. I do know my father had had a pseudo marriage. His first wife wasn't divorced from her first husband.

Gussie's mother was Indian. Her father was a sea islander. All of her siblings were good looking. She was the third oldest girl, and the third best looker. Aunt Della, as the story goes, was gorgeous. She died the year after I was born. Aunt Josephine was the oldest. She was the one with the most color; two shades under high yellow. I never saw a blemish on her face, and I knew her about forty-five years. She was beautiful.

I don't adhere to signs, but both of my aunts married Scorpio men. Aunt Josephine and Aunt Mattie married men who were shorter, very possessive, bossy and fussy. They were also family men. If it had not been for Aunt Jo's husband, none of us would have been here from the South.

He fussed, but loved deeply. He just wanted to be the "head". They, the Scorpio men, did most of the shopping, chose the houses to live in, put up curtains, etc. My stepfather was also a Scorpio. Born on the same day as my mom, but two years later. It was a struggle for her to keep it a secret from Willie that she was older. It wasn't the thing to do in those years.

Murphy and Gussie loved each other with the passion of youth. I wonder if they would have chosen each other if they had been exposed to a broader community. You see I chose Grandpa Alex after looking at many different people in my denomination, school, work, community and friends of my friends and family. Grandma Gussie was in a small country town. She adapted to that life because that was all she knew. They worked, played, lived and loved hard. Her father was not a drinker nor smoker, and he didn't marry women who did those things. So, she didn't pick up those habits. She thought she was too cute to dip snuff.

My dad was the typical southern macho-man. He was the happy-go-lucky survive-aholic . . . by any means necessary" for my family, bootlegging, and stealing hogs and chickens from the White man (which they didn't really think was stealing). They knew they weren't getting paid their worth, so they had no conscience—it really belonged to them. So, Murphy and his brother-in-law were notorious for stealing from other plantations. His plantation boss protected him if he got caught. The plantation boss took care of other crimes also. In the thirties I don't know if the farm was called a plantation (a rose by any other name is still a rose). My family lived on T. C. Outlaw's place. I don't understand it, but one of my great-uncles was named after this "place boss". His name was T. C. Thomton. He wasn't fair-skinned so he wasn't biologically T. C's.

That's why many older Black folks had initials for their first name, with no apparent corresponding names, (i.e. T. C. could have been Thomas Charles) but what did they know. The reason some names were Bobby, Billie, or Willie is because they didn't know that it was supposed to be Robert or William. No older Black man that I know was called Dick for Richard. No Black woman was called Betty for Elizabeth or Peggy for Margaret, etc. Their real names were just Belly or Peggy. Only our men had initials because White women didn't (they were Miss Sally Jane, Mary Sue or Rita Mae, etc.).

Gussie and Murphy fought. He didn't beat her per se; they were tit-for-tat. One night he must have gotten the best of her and fell asleep. He snored and slept with his mouth open. Gussie was so mad (not angry), that she boiled a teakettle full of water and was ready to pour it down his throat. His hog-stealing partner/brother-in-law caught and stopped her short of mutilating, if not killing, her husband.

One day Murphy told Gussie and his youngest sister Jessie not to leave the house. Well Gussie refused to be tamed and bossed. She was liberated even in the 1930's. Well, Murphy thought he'd scare them. He took a shotgun and shot over their heads. His oldest sister, Rosie, had been unable to walk for years. She was so scared she got up and ran, never to be paralyzed again! These are stories we laugh about now, but were very serious and true when they were happening.

In January 1937, Murphy had to sneak his family (Gussie and me) out of Mississippi because of some trouble he had gotten into. No one ever said what the trouble was. We moved in with Aunt Josephine and Uncle Cally. His name was Humphrey Calhoun, but he and Aunt Jo called each other Cally. His name was Humphrey with the "H", but he insisted that the H was silent. He said his name was Umphrey, like humble was umble.

Uncle Cally got Murphy a job at Victor Chemical where he worked for almost forty years. Gussie was a housewife. She was very clean and he taught her to cook. I don't remember my mother washing on a rub board or mopping the floor on her knees, but I know I was always clean and so was the house. I was never hungry. Beds were always made and clothes always hung up. But I don't remember her doing it. Maybe she did it at night; that's when I like doing my work.

I remember visiting our family, her cousin's and sibling's house. I was her only child and I was with her most of the time. We even ran away together. We'd stay away a week or two. Until she went to Ohio and stayed so long that Murphy replaced her.

Gussie knew that she and Murphy were from two different worlds. There's a saying, "You can take the person out of the country, but you can't take the country out of the person". Well, the country never got out of Murphy and, strangely enough, the country was never in Gussie. She wanted another life. She looked for it. She felt that she deserved it. She was like a princess displaced.

Water was seeking it's own level. She met Willie who owned a small business in East Chicago Heights. He was married. He grew up Pentecostal. When he was eighteen, he met a woman who was thirty-eight, a missionary in his church. She was his first sexual experience. They got married. I don't know which was first. They were married about ten years. He was the

Assistant Pastor at his church. They owned a beautiful house and had the only bus to run from Chicago Heights to East Chicago Heights.

That's how Gussie met Willie. He drove the bus. One thing led to another. Murphy cut up one time too many. Gussie left for the last time. Willie wanted a younger woman. She was the right color, but the wrong religion. I have a saying that my sons hate, "The dumbest woman is smarter than the smartest man"! Then I ask them to prove me wrong with their life. I tell them ever since Adam, women have been able to determine man's actions. Samson couldn't lay his head in a lady's lap without divulging all his secrets. David, a man after God's own heart, couldn't stand to see a woman take a bath. Solomon, the wisest man who ever lived, married and had 1,000 women. Most men can't take care of one woman. In our lifetime, a King denounced his throne for a woman. We know several preachers who have lost their empires for a "piece" or a peek. Politicians also. There are powerful men who were felled by women. The most powerful women look for men who would have as much to loose as they. Many men, because of ego maybe, look for weak, powerless, pitiful women who have nothing to lose if they are exposed and everything to gain. I don't ask you to agree with my theory, just watch it.

So, Gussie got Willie. He lost, and left his wife, house, bus company, church, family and friends. Her family was against it, but they were not anti-divorce like Willie's family. You'd stay in a bad marriage to save face. So. Gussie gained a man who was educated, city born and bred, and with a different set of values. The only fight they had was for the backside of the bed when someone died. Gussie was an astute student. Willie was the proverbial teacher. His first wife taught him everything. But, here was a beautiful lady who he could teach. Darn it! She was someone else's wife and had a child, but what the heck! The child could stay with the father.

Willie never mistreated me. He wanted me to call him Dad, or Pops, or something other than Mr. Willie. By then, they had moved to Chicago and had been accepted by a church. He was the Superintendent of Sunday school, a great teacher. Dad finally gave in and let me spend some weekends and part of the summer with them. We studied the lessons together. He didn't want his family to come short in the answering department so we were all versed. He could wake us up and ask us any question and we knew the answer. No one at the church knew that I was a stepdaughter. That's why I couldn't call him Mr. Willie. I was about two shades darker than he was and if they thought anything, they would have thought she was my stepmother.

I mention color only for description. Color was never important to my family, just to my stepfather's family. They said we should marry a light-skinned person because we should think of the children, Well, I have seen some beautiful coal black people and I've seen some not so attractive light-skinned people. Somewhere along the line, my father (Murphy) taught me that "beauty is as beauty does". He embraced the comedian's saying, "Beauty was skin deep, but ugly was to the bone". He admonished me to be beautiful on the inside and to be pleasant all the time. To keep my nasty feelings to myself and work them out.

That's why I never allowed moodiness in our house. If you came out into the general population, you were going to be decent. If not, you can go back to your room until you can get it together. Just because you are miserable, don't make everyone else that way. When you find a way to talk to us with a civil tongue, let's talk. I gave the kids a chance to talk to me and tell me almost anything, but they had to be respectful. They could not holler at me. Barry was so frustrated several times. I bent that rule and let him scream and holler.

Willie gave Mother the kind of life she always aspired to. He was very sociable and she was a perfect hostess. When a visiting minister would come to the church, he would invite him home. We rubbed elbows with the hierarchy of the church evangelists, superintendents, and bishops. One of their guests frightened me. His landlord had shot him in the face. In 1950 I don't know how widespread plastic surgery was, but this man didn't, or couldn't, take advantage of it. He was disfigured. His nose was kind of to the side, among other things. My mother basked in this glory. She loved her handsome, intelligent, ambitious, personable husband. She learned to fish, but she hated fishing so I would fish with Willie. She and her sister-in-law would cook the fish and fix a picnic.

After the scandal died down, Willie's family accepted Mother with open arms. She never smoked or drank. So, all she had to do was slop wearing make-up, lower her dresses, lengthen her sleeves and learn the jargon of the "church". Willie's youngest sister is seven months older than I am. We were in the same grade. I met her in the seventh grade. She took me under her wing. We ate lunch together. We fasted on Tuesday's and Friday's. I didn't know why, but she said the "church" didn't eat on those days. So, I complied since I had started going to the church, It was a small town of 25,000 people so everyone knew who I was. But that didn't seem to matter to me then. Later on when it was dating time, the mothers wanted girls from a good family or someone who had been several generations in the church. The theory was; "It's better to have a good girl gone bad than a bad girl gone good".

The good girl gone bad would revert to what she knows in a crisis and vice versa. I proved them wrong. I assumed some values that, after a time, became my own. They worked for me. Crisis only made me dig in deeper. Not to the church, but to God. I think I was partially responsible for my mother being saved, Willie was very strict. He didn't want her to drink coffee. Gussie was a Perkins by birth and they were notorious coffee drinkers. She was addicted. She became a "closet coffee drinker." They were so funny. Now that I think about it, they not only fought for the backside of the bed, but they fought about coffee too. She'd buy it and hide it. When he went to work, she would perk and drink it. He'd come home and, like a bloodhound, sniff it out. She couldn't have a coffeepot. So, she did it the old fashioned way by boiling water, pulling in the grinds, putting a top on it, and letting it steep for several minutes. The grinds would go to the bottom and, using a strainer, you would have a good cup of coffee. It you like it strong, you add more coffee. She liked it almost thick enough for a spoon to stand in it (a slight exaggeration).

Willie always had the kind of jobs where he could pop in at anytime, and he did. Willie and Mother used to dress alike many times. He had them five suits apiece tailored that were identical material. He bought her fur coats and jewelry. She wore fancy hats and high-heeled shoes. She wore high-heeled shoes until eighteen days before she died in 1983. She was a fancy lady. The princess found her prince.

There were nine children in Willie's family. He always wanted children. I was sort of a thorn because he thought I wanted my parent's back together. He didn't understand that I suggested the separation. He didn't understand that when my parents were together, I had two bad parents. After they remarried, I ended up with four good ones.

Well, Mother got more involved with the church. She got pregnant at about age thirty-eight, but it was in her tubes. She had to have surgery and one tube was removed. She was really sick for awhile. That's why she was at my aunt's house to receive the call from my first fiancée's ex-wife. After the surgery, things seemed to get back to normal, but that was just on the surface. Mother's best friend said she was pregnant by Willie. Mother took that as a sign that she was reaping what she sowed, even though she wasn't a friend to Willie's ex-wife. She felt she couldn't be saved and stay in the situation since she had gotten him wrong. He begged her to stay.

My aunt never knew why I left her house. I gave a three-month notice that I was going back to school full-time and back to live with my father. Mother had shared with me that she had to leave Willie. That, in good conscience, she couldn't stay. The best friend wasn't pregnant, but he had been there. Mother dished it out, but she couldn't take it.

Mother moved back to Chicago Heights to Aunt Josephine's house. Willie begged her on hands and knees to return to him, but she wouldn't. Neither one of them ever had a good relationship afterwards. I think they could have stayed together and worked it out. I found him in Alabama about five years before he died. We talked on the phone several times and corresponded. I loved him; he was one of my two fathers.

Murphy's last wife was young and light skinned with curly hair and she loved him and all of his family; including his extended family which was my mother's family. Gussie had never worked to speak of. She might have done a little in the war plants, but her husbands were good providers. Queenie didn't have to work either. She was good to me. She is my last mother and is still alive. When my sister Alice died, I had siblings come to the funeral from two mothers. Five from Mother Doll and four from Mother Queenie and me from Mother Gussie. It was a great family reunion. A time of bonding this blended family and love.

# CHAPTER THIRTEEN

I was a member of the Portland Street Church, the same church where Willie was the Assistant Pastor when he left with mother. When she came back to town, she put her membership there, and stayed there in good standing until she moved to Minnesota in 1967. She was friendly with Murphy, but he was more like a family member. If they entertained the thought of reconciliation, I didn't know about it.

When Alex and I got married, Gussie was renting the top part of a duplex from her mother's sister. Alex and I moved in with her. In about three weeks, we found a two-bedroom apartment, so she moved with us. She lived with us about two months. When my cousin had problems, Mother was the most logical one to take my cousins five children. She fostered them for about three years (1959 to 1962).

There were several times during the years when my children were small that I might have needed help, but I only asked for it when I was in dire straits. I bartered for things. If the kids and I spent the night with Grandma Gussie or Daddy Murphy, I'd help cook or clean, maybe wash or go to the store.

A funny thing happened when Mother took the kids. She moved in a big house in East Chicago Heights. Daddy and Queenie's house was on the next block. The only thing that separated them and their back doors was a field. Queenie's children would come over and play with, and help with, Mother's foster children.

Grandma Gussie finally gave the kids to their father. I think people did this in the olden days. That was hard, but she moved in with me so she wouldn't be lonely. My mother and my husband tolerated each other. Grandpa Alex was a cut-up when he was younger. She didn't like how he treated me or the children. One time she said, "Seeing what you are going through, I could have stayed with either one of my husbands"!

Grandpa Alex was not the provider that my two fathers were. He liked rewarding himself, and others, on Fridays after work. Sometimes most of his money was gone when he got home Saturday mornings. For almost one year, I was depressed. I didn't know it then, but in retrospect that's where I was. I got hooked on soap operas. I was confined to the house because, by this time, I had four children and the oldest was only six. One was sick and my husband was a weekend alcoholic. I would get up at six a.m. to fix breakfast and lunch for Alex and send him to work. I would clean up and put on dinner. I'd cook breakfast for the kids and take my bath, pray and read the Bible. The kids would get up at ten a.m. (they were good sleepers). I'd do my routine with them. A bath a day was a must.

I'd sit on the couch from 12:00 p.m. to 3:00 p.m. and watch the soaps, just getting up during commercials to do necessary things. This inactivity caused me to gain a lot of weight. Alex needed to unwind when he got home, so I scheduled the kids' naps at 3:30. We all, including Alex, went to bed at 3:30 in the afternoon and slept till 5:30. We got up and ate around 6:00. We then talked and played, or watched TV until 10:00 at night, when it was time to go to bed. If I went to church, he kept the kids and they went to bed on time. I didn't go to church on Friday nights unless I took all the kids, because nine and three-quarters times out of ten Alex wouldn't be home, Well, Grandma Gussie hated this. Plus, she didn't like the way Grandpa Alex disciplined the kids. These were the sons she never had and was very protective of. I was in the middle of two opinionated people. By this time, Mother was working for Catholic Charities.

One day, I got a phone call from one of my friends who had an alcoholic husband. Mine was just a weekend alkie. She asked me to look out of the door to see if he was in the parking lot near my house. Indeed he was. He had just picked up his check and she didn't want him to spend it. I went over to the lot and brought him to the house. I literally pulled him away from his drinking buddies. I sat him at the kitchen table and poured coffee and food into him. Well, I was continuing my routine of cooking supper before the kids got up, so I made cornbread. I hadn't been in this house long. My other stove lit automatically. I turned this stove on to preheat before I made the cornbread. When I started to put the bread in the stove, I realized it wasn't hot. Then I remembered it didn't light automatically. Well, I had been preoccupied with witnessing to my friend. I turned the oven off, got a match, turned the oven back on, struck the match, and was blown into another room. My face and arm were burned. My friend sobered up right away and took me to the hospital. He had been driving in that condition. When I got to the hospital, I had first, second, and third degree burns. My eyelashes and brows were singed off. I had burns from my nose, down. My right arm was burned from the shoulder to the wrist. They treated me, and sent me home with Codeine. I can't remember if it was Tylenol 3 or not. Mother, working for Catholic Charities, got them to send in a lady for six weeks to care for the children and me. She would spend four or five hours a day helping.

I used cocoa butter on my face and arm. When my face cleared up, I stopped using it. I wore long-sleeved dresses anyway, I reasoned, so what the heck. Who would see it? I was just glad to be alive and not disfigured. My friend stayed sober about one year after that incident. Shortly after that is when we had to move to Minnesota for Barry's schooling. This incident is partially the reason I don't fry much. I hate grease popping on me. It also made me more determined not to go to hell. Fire must be the worst death. I was miserable for at least two weeks. The pills got me through.

I believe in divine healing, but I have a low tolerance for pain. Byron was about three months old when this happened. Well, around Christmas time I was hanging curtains and fixing up the house. I felt the same problem that I felt in junior high school when I had the missionary pray for me, like my womb had fallen. To get through Christmas, I took the rest of the Codeine pills. In about one week I started fainting. I went to church and fainted. They prayed and I fainted again, three times all together. They called Mother and Alex. They took me to the hospital. My blood count had gone down to five; it's supposed to be fourteen. They started me on blood transfusions. On the third pint of blood, I began to have giant chills. I was dying. So, I had a talk with God. I'm not afraid of dying I just don't like pain. I asked Him to heal me or take me. We made an agreement that day. By the next day, twenty-four hours later, I was sitting up in bed. The doctor said that I could go home the next day. He also said I would have to take B12 shots for the rest of my life.

I left the hospital and went to church. They were in revival and had been praying for me. I believed I was healed. I took one B12 shot. I'm fine. That's been thirty-two years ago. I have had no reoccurrence of anemia.

Thank God that AIDS wasn't contaminating blood in those days, at least we didn't know about it. I was sick on New Year's Day of 1967. In October of 1967 we moved to Minnesota.

The house we moved into was the biggest I had ever seen. The house was built in a "U" shape. The front room, dining room, and kitchen were on the left side near Highway 55 on James Avenue North. The bathroom was in the middle, then a hallway to the bedroom. When you came off the street, you came into a large rotunda with stairs leading upstairs. The house might have been a one-family dwelling at one time. So our apartment was around this rotunda. If you were in the living room, you couldn't hear what was going on in the bedrooms.

My mother and husband moved here before the New Year of 1968. The winters of '67 and '68 were cold, but different. It didn't feel cold. I would take the garbage out in short sleeves. Before I knew it, I had pneumonia. The medical profession said exposure did not cause the pneumonia. I don't know. I just know I was sick. But, I learned to respect Minnesota winters that first year. I remember a blue fake fur coat I got that was the warmest coat I have ever had. I didn't like fur because I looked like a bear in them. I couldn't wear pants because it was against my religion. That's one of the values that work for me. I no longer think it's a sin; I just think I shouldn't break my record. I've never worn a pair in sixty-two years, why start now? In my opinion, some women should not wear pants. You can see all the cellulite. A skirt hides more flab. I have noticed that ladies get looser when they wear pants—legs all opened. Is that old fashioned of me?

I like men to let me on the elevators first, open doors, and pull out chairs for me. My sons still hold out their arms for me to hold on to. Grandpa Alex is a gentleman. After he got the run out of him, he became an excellent husband. He's never hit nor cursed me. I wouldn't handle that. He had to learn early on in our marriage that hollering at me only made my mind go blank. If he commanded or demanded anything from me, I couldn't have done it if I wanted to. He learned that being nice to me made me bend over backwards to accommodate.

Grandpa Alex got a job at a car place in Southeast Minneapolis. He had to walk several days because his schedule was different than the buses. It was cold, but he walked so his family could eat. He left there and went to a large department store, from there to General Electric. When they downsized his department, his department head personally recommended him beginning at a neighboring factory, General Motors. He worked there until retirement.

Grandma Gussie didn't like the way Grandpa Alex disciplined the children. In many ways they were more alike than he and I. They liked to study the Bible together. They were both spiffy dressers. They knew "worldly" singers and performers. They both had been to the Regal Theater in Chicago to see Mom's Mabley and Redd Foxx. She said she danced with Redd Foxx at the Black & Tan Tavern in Chicago Heights in the Forties. They both had won dancing contests at nightclubs; I'd never been to a nightclub. In fact, when I came to Minnesota I had to adjust to eating in places where liquor was served.

When I started work at TCOIC (Twin Cities Opportunity and Industrialization Center) in 1968, going to lunch with the gang was challenging. I had been taught not to "sit in the seat of the scornful" and to "love not the world or the things in the world". Going to bars was worldly in my opinion. I had to come to grips with the fact that liquor wasn't going to contaminate me unless it got on the inside of me. We didn't go out much back home. If we did, it was mostly take-out barbecue or chicken. We had several soul food restaurants, but they didn't serve alcohol.

I was the buffer between these two people I loved (Mother and Alex). Ninety percent of the time, we had a pleasant home life. Grandpa Alex went on and off the wagon for years. He finally gave it up about nine years before she died. When he would give up drinking, he wouldn't go through treatment, and he didn't know how to handle it cold turkey. We liked him better drinking. He was irritable when he was dry, and very nervous. The kids had to be really quiet, or he would go off. Then one day he'd come in happy. He'd fallen off the wagon. Barry was so scared of him that he would be calmly sitting on the steps, but when he'd hear the car motor, he'd run upstairs to his bedroom. Grandma Gussie learned to resent him strongly. She cooked foods he liked. One of his favorite meals was rabbit and dumplings. (I don't eat Thumper, Bambi or Donald). He liked all of her food, but her pork chops. She made them taste like beef jerky. Pork had to be well done.

One day, when Barton was about thirteen, it was the straw that broke the camel's back. We were at church. Barton was behind the church smoking. One of the older ministers caught him and told Alex. Barton threatened the old man (I'm sure he was about seventy) and Alex slapped him. Barton's jaw was cracked. Alex is a large, not fat, man with huge hands. I took Barton to a doctor and tried to get him to report it. He said it was not abuse (in 1973), just an unlucky punch. He asked Barton how it had happened. Because Alex had not hit him but once, and with an opened hand, it was not abuse. Barton's jaw was wired for six weeks. He stayed at Mother's house for those six weeks.

I left Alex for three and a half weeks. I was gone for good. I had learned how to drive two years before, but I would only get my permit renewed. I gave Alex a month's notice that I was leaving him. One day I came home and couldn't get in the house. I had to climb through the window. Alex was inside asleep. When I got in I woke him up. His eyes were blood red. I got scared and knew I couldn't live like that any more. I had to make a plan. I was going home to Daddy Murphy. I was taking the car and the kids. My friend's mother asked someone with a license to go with me to help drive. I was going, even if I had to go alone! I left Grandma Gussie and Grandpa Alex here in Minnesota, in two different houses.

Grandpa Murphy let me stay in Chicago Heights for one week. He heard my story, let me cool off, and then gave me money to go back to Minnesota. I was hurt. My father should have understood. That was the second time he let me down where a man was involved. I called my prayer partner in Michigan. I went there and we stayed two and a half weeks. My friend from home called me and told me that Alex had passed out on the doctor's table. He had been getting several different prescriptions filled from different doctors for his back injury. We came home and stayed with Alex for about one week, then I found the kids and I a house. I was really through. Mother was in her place, Alex was in his, and the kids and I in ours. If I had believed in divorce, this would have been the time.

# CHAPTER FOURTEEN

Big Ma used to suck the mucus out of my nose when I was a baby because they hadn't invented, to our knowledge, a nasal aspirator. She loved me enough not to let me die. Oh, I'm so glad for that invention because I don't know if I could have done that for any of you.

I pray that your parents stay healthy because I am not a good baby sitter. I took care of my babies. I was the best mother I could be. In fact, if I rated myself, I'd be an eight. I love having all of you at my house. I love cooking for you and having family get-togethers, but I want your parents to take you home when they leave. I think some of them stay until I traditionally put them out, sometimes at 3 am. Some of them wait until I say, "Okay, it's time to go home".

The majority of you have stayed with us at different times, but your parents were there also. I took care of my kids. Sometimes my feet didn't touch ground for six weeks at a time. I paid my dues. I don't want to take that privilege away from your parents. It is a privilege because you grow up so fast, and you wonder where the years went. God has entrusted you in the care of your parents. They have an awesome responsibility to show, teach, love and protect you. I don't want to take this away from them.

One day I looked around and I had thirteen people and two dogs, a Doberman and a German Shepherd, living in my house. We had three bedrooms and a finished basement. I couldn't find a quiet place to read. I had to go outside and sit in the car to read. That day I made up my mind to move into an apartment. Milton took the house, and Alex and I moved with a bedroom set, a couch, chair, table, two plates, two cups, two saucers, one pot, one pan, one skillet, two forks, two spoons, two knives, one TV, a radio, towels, sheets, and our clothes. I needed space. We have lived here twelve years. Even though it has gotten crowded at times, I have never regretted the move.

Someone asked me one day why older people sleep in separate beds. I can only speak from my experience. Two years ago I had pneumonia, with a deep cough. Alex thought he would sleep in our other bedroom. After about two weeks, he fell in love with the mattress and the quietness. I like to listen to music, or try to learn a language in my sleep. I don't like the fan, and he does. It made more sense to use both bedrooms. If we get an out-of-town guest and we don't use the guest apartment in our building, we will give them one of our rooms. When someone's in town, the woman will have to sleep with me, and the man with Alex. That has cut company down considerably. No one wants to stay here under these circumstances.

Sometimes I will lay in his bed and watch the religious station. He doesn't have cable in there; or he will watch TV with me. There is no phone in Grandpa's room and that's why he likes it . . . peace and quiet with him, his TV, his Bible, books and his fan.

There was a barbecue shack right off of the alley on Fifteenth and Wentworth. Uncle George's property ran by Mr. Horse Kelly (I think it must have been Horace). Horse Kelly used to barbecue pig snoots (noses), tails, feet, ears, ribs, rabbits, coons, and possums, etc. He had a thriving business because he was within a foot of two bars and a half block from the American Legion, which also sold liquor. It was rumored that fat meat coated your stomach so the alcohol wouldn't "burn" through it. In 1945 most of the people on the East Side of Chicago Heights didn't have refrigeration. I don't know why we weren't all ptomaine poisoned. We had iceboxes. We bought ice from the iceman every other day. They came in twenty-five, fifty, seventy-five, or one hundred-pound blocks. If you wanted fifty pounds, you would put a card in the window with the number fifty on top. Daddy taught me how to freshen up the not-so-fresh meat. I would soak it in salt, soda, and vinegar. When it quit foaming, I would rinse it and cook it. We were never sick from food poisoning. I bet you Mr. Horse Kelly used those same methods.

We had grease cans. We saved bacon grease. That's what we fried with. When it would become rancid, we would boil a potato in the grease and strain it. It would be as good as new. Even fish grease could be purified. The potato absorbs the taste. During the war, we were asked to save our grease. Volunteers would come and collect it every so often. We also had ration stamps for sugar, meat, and gas. There were other things too, but I can't remember. Each person in your family got a book of stamps. I remember trading sugar for meat. I can't prove it, but I believe I ate horsemeat during the war. It's hard to tell the difference between beef and horse.

We ate a boiled dinner every day. Collards, mustard, turnips, or wild greens, pinto, navy, great northern, lime (butter) beans, black-eyed peas, green beans, white potatoes, and cabbage. We didn't eat red beans and rice and we only used kidney beans for chili. For seasoning we used ham hocks or salt pork. That was usually our meat until Sundays. On Sundays we might have fried salt pork. Slice the fat back, boil it for a few minutes, pour off the water and then fry it. Doing this, you eliminate some of the salt and little of the fat. It was cheaper than bacon. A typical breakfast was meat, eggs, grits, biscuits, coffee and milk. Sometimes the meat would be pork chops, steak or chicken. And sometimes the grits would be rice. I never heard of potatoes for breakfast until I was an adult.

Our salads were seasoning with salt, pepper and vinegar. Maybe that's why we didn't get sick. We used a lot of vinegar, hot peppers, garlic and onions. Aunt Josephine, Mother's oldest sister taught me to love garlic. She would cook a pork roast with many cloves of garlic pressed into the meat. The garlic taste permeated the roast. I am eighty-five percent vegetarian. Maybe I have eaten my share of meat in my day. One day I was thawing some hamburger in the microwave and the bowl was full of blood. I began to think, "Hmm, au jus is just cooked blood". Ick! Sometimes I taste the blood in the meat, so I give it up for several weeks, six or eight. Then I can eat and be full, but feel like I'm starving. I will then eat some red meat and the feeling goes away after several meals. So I am on about two months, off about two months and on chicken and fish for two months. I eat whatever I want for two months then start the cycle again.

We used to have silk stockings during the war. I was too young for them. We had to wear nylon. We bought Kentucky Lump coal to heat our potbelly stoves. We had a gas burning cooking stove, but no central heat or hot water. We had to heat water on the stove for dishes, washing and bathing. We "washed up" every day and bathed every Saturday in a number three tub. In retrospect, I bet we gave off quite a whiff.

I was made to wear snuggies to school. I was ashamed. I didn't want to be seen in them in gym. Now I order them from Lane Bryant to get through these Minnesota winters. So, I took them off in the coal shed before school and put them back on to return home from school. We had our form of rebellion fifty years ago too! I had no idea what television, microwave ovens, ball point pens, pantyhose or clothes dryers were.

We used the same number-three bathtub to wash clothes in. The only air conditioning that I knew was in the movies. We didn't have penicillin, any polio vaccine, nor fast food or frozen food. Can you imagine no credit cards? We actually got thirteen donuts . . . that's the "bakers dozen". Banks were opened from 9 a.m. to 2 p.m . . . . that's the "banker's hours". There were no VCR's, CD's, cassette tapes or players. We had 78's, then 33 1/3 and 45's for records.

Our Coca-Cola was in six ounce bottles, not twelve and sixteen ounce or liters. Yogurt was called clabbered milk, which tastes good with hot cornbread. There were no househusbands unless he had a peg leg or a hook for a hand. Phone calls were a nickel and you could mail a letter for about two cents. But, you could work all day for about five dollars. Those were the "good old days". Some folk wish for their return; not me. Give me hot running water so I can soak in an enamel bathtub at least once a day. Let me freeze my leftovers so I can eat them whenever I want to. I cook by "spells". When I feel like it, I will buy ten bunches of greens, cook and freeze them in small freezer bags and eat them as desired once a week for a month.

My bedroom was so cold when I was a child, I had to sleep with a double blanket and three homemade (hand made) quilts. Sometimes they were so heavy I could hardly turn over. Our cat slept on my feet . . . time brings about a change. I love animals in their own habitat, not mine. It just occurred to me that you might not know what a double blanket was. Imagine your blanket twice the length with no seam at the foot. You sleep on the bottom half and cover with the top. Your feet can't get out.

There were outhouses in East Chicago Heights (now called Ford Heights) until about 1958, and also pumps. In 1944 Aunt Josephine and Uncle Cally lived at 1000 Lexington Avenue. They had rose bushes in the front yard. On the south side was First Union Baptist Church. There was a driveway and a pigpen on the northeast side. Due north was a large garden and right behind the house was an enclosed chicken and geese yard. We had to go through this yard to get to the outhouse. I hate walking on chicken and goose manure. It tickles my feet. The geese were mean. They would run after you and bite you if they caught you. I had two first cousins that stayed most of the time with Aunt Josephine because their mother had died from childbirth complications. Carol Jean was Burnette's sister. We called him Junior. Carol Jean was seven, Burnette was nine and I was eight. We were a team. I had no siblings growing up with me so these were my sister and brother.

Carol was going to the outhouse one day and the geese got after her. They didn't attack because they couldn't catch her. She ran so fast that she fell into the manure up to her neck. What a sight and what a smell! The first book I read in the 5th grade was <u>God's Little Acre</u>. Then I was turned on to Pearl S. Buck. I read all of her books I could find. I learned I could travel to many countries by reading.

My first religious novel was <u>In His Steps</u> by Charles M. Sheldon. I was 14 and tried to pattern my life after that plan, following in Jesus' steps and when in doubt asking what would Jesus do in similar situations. Reading is my past time.

My grandmother and I would sit on the porch and shuck corn, shell peas or beans, snap green beans, prepare the greens for washing, and peel peaches and apples for preserves and jelly. I didn't know this was work. This was our lifestyle. This was what we did. I was never bored.

Somehow I always had a sense of self. I can't ever remember not accepting myself. I never wanted to be White or light skinned. I made the best of my weight. I looked good all the time. I washed and ironed my clothes, washed by body and changed my underwear everyday. I never had a problem with friends because I was a beautiful person. Ruby was beautiful inside; wrinkles, gray hair or walking on a cane will never change that.

One day at work someone asked me if I liked lobster. I had just seen someone cook one on the "Today Show". I told them, "No, they squeal when you cook them". That wise person asked me what did I think that a pig was doing when they killed him. I remember Poppa killing a hog at Aunt Josephine's. I had fed her slop and given her water. I went and watched her nurse her babies. She was real to me; almost like a pet. Well, when the piglets were weaned Poppa isolated this hog and fed her good food for about two or three weeks. She was put up on a wood stage where she couldn't wallow in the mud. I think they fed her lye to clean her out. This was called the fattening pen. On killing day, some of the neighbors came to help Poppa kill his hog. You have never heard such squealing, piercing or agonizing cries. So what's the difference? The little noise the live lobster makes when she is boiled alive, or the noise the hog makes when she is being killed; whether she was shot in the head or had her throat cut.

I tried to kill a chicken on day. I took him by the neck and swung him around like I had seen my grandmother do. My hands started tingling and I dropped her. She started jumping all over the yard. I had injured her, but not broken her neck. Someone else had to come and complete the job. When chickens were acting sick, just lying around, my grandfather and I would go to the chicken yard and check their tongues. They would have something hard on it. He would take it off and the chicken would get better. He called it a pip.

Rhubarb would grow every year. Carol, Junior and I would get a stalk and eat it with salt, fresh from the garden and with no washing. I wouldn't do that today. One of my favorite pies is Strawberry Rhubarb.

We loved climbing fruit trees. Cherry trees were my favorite. Apples were my least favorite. You had to be careful; they could give you a bad tummy ache. I ate pears, peaches, plums fresh from the trees, strawberries, and grapes from their vines and bushes.

Miss Willis used to lake us fishing. She was the first person I had heard of to take in foster children. In fact, I had never heard the term "foster". She would have two or three foster sons. They would be in our church and in our schools until it was time for them to leave. We never treated them any different than the others in the neighborhood. Who could talk? Many of our families were fragmented. Miss Willis took us to the creek about a mile away. I remember not only catching fish and craw daddies, but also drinking from the running brook. Miss Willis showed me where it was safe to drink. Afterwards, I thought, "How safe can it be; someone upstream could have peed in this creek". When we didn't go fishing we would sit under the weeping willow tree and talk. I can't imagine me sitting under that tree now, as afraid as I am of snakes.

Uncle George Range, my great uncle, was retired when I first met him. He owned a lot of property; a cab company, barber shop, church, restaurant, apartment building, and several houses. He was separated from his wife, Aunt Mickey, but they lived next door to each other until he died. Neither one of them ever married again. They had five children, three girls and two boys. I would go to his house on Saturdays and clean for him and he would give me an allowance. He didn't believe in giving you something for nothing.

I liked older people, so I would visit Uncle Joe Range, my grandmothers oldest brother, her sister's Aunt Georgia Wilson and Aunt Mattie Early. They were Indians from Mississippi. They kept their private lives private. Aunt Georgia had only one husband. Aunt Mattie had two, but they were both dead. She was a property owner too. She rented a room to a blind man named Ed Scales. We called him Uncle Ed. We had to put a handle to his name. He baby sat Carol, Junior and me. We three tried to terrorize him, but after he spanked us twice, we calmed down and the four of us became fast friends.

Uncle Ed would take a bus from Chicago Heights to Chicago Proper to go to school and then to work. He made beautiful belts, suspenders, wallets and purses. One day he reached under the sink and got a box of soap and I said, "Uncle Ed, I think you can see"! Then Carol and Junior started laughing and agreeing. He had a razor strap that he sharpened his straight razor on. Uncle Ed went right to this strap and promptly whipped all three of us. I can't remember him leaving any marks. I don't think he was angry, but one time he was really angry. We wasted some kind of oil on the floor and he fell. We got it then too.

I never heard him curse. We peeked and peered to see if anything was going on between Aunt Mattie Early and Uncle Ed. We didn't even see them touch. We never heard a rumor, even to this day. She was an usher at Union Evangelistic Baptist Church and later at Calvary Baptist. Her reputation was impeccable. From her first marriage she had two stepdaughters, Ethel Lee and Fannie Mae, and from them she had six grandchildren. They were her only children. I wouldn't have known they were stepchildren but by their color. Aunt Mattie was very fair skinned with straight black hair down past her waist. Her daughters were not mixed. I was one of those question-asking kids (was Byron like me?), and got many answers! Step, half, foster, or adopted didn't mean anything in my family. A relative was a relative.

I had fun in church. In Bible study we were very competitive about who did the most research. Choir rehearsal was fun also. Have you heard recordings where you didn't quite get the words? Well, Mary Ann said, "A few more risings I'll be setting on the sun". It was, "A few more risings and settings of the sun". She also said, "There's not a friend like the long legged Jesus". It was supposed to be "lonely Jesus". Marie said, "When my feet get cold, my eyes are shut, my body's been chilled by the hands of death, my arm's glued to the roof of my mouth, my tongue lay folded across my breast, but you don't have to worry about the way I left. The Lord promised to met me there". By the time she got to "you don't have to worry", we were crying because we were suppressing the laughter!

Grandma Gussie ate her greens with her original utensils, her fingers. Can you imagine this beautiful princess squishing greens, cornbread, cut up onions, tomatoes and hot peppers between her fingers and putting it in her mouth? Well, imagine it. She wouldn't eat greens with a fork. It skipped a generation. Eating greens like that is like walking on goose manure in a chicken yard to me, but one of my children eats it like that. Guess who? Aunt Josephine washed each green leaf separately. We had to pick them and shake any bugs or worms off the greens first. Then they were soaked in salt to kill any bugs that the eye had missed. Daddy's side of the family washed them from sink to pan as many times as necessary to rid the greens of grit, then one more time for good measure.

I wondered why we weren't bothered with mosquitoes. Then I remembered our smoke outs in our yard. We would gather up old rags and burn them at dusk; not really burn . . . they sort of smoldered. The smoke kept away the unwanted critters. We'd sit around talking, telling tales, eating peanuts, which had been dried, on top of the house, or eating sweet potatoes which had been cooked in the ashes of the fireplace. There were ashes in the potato, but they were good. I don't know why we didn't die from the things we took and ate.

Did you know hogshead cheese was made from a real hogshead? Do you think eyes and all? I thought it was just a name. I have since realized that headcheese was not ours originally, and that every ethnic group has something gross in their menu or diet. We might eat chitterlings. I have cooked them four times in forty years of marriage. Grandpa doesn't like mine. Some groups eat blood pudding, blood sausage and drink warm blood fresh from the animal. Some groups eat an unborn chicken fresh from the egg. One lady came in the store where I worked and asked for cheese with worms in it. Limburger cheese stinks. Tripe is cow stomach lining. Some people make hot tamales out of pig ears, tails and feet, among other things. Have you seen that commercial about hot dogs when the butcher says, "You don't want to know what's in it"? Some cultures cook chicken soup with chicken feet and the rooster's head with the beak and comb (that little red thing).

So, don't be ashamed of your culture. Don't be ashamed of who you are. Some of you are passing for something else, but you'd better research that something else. Every culture has the good and bad. It's up to you whether you're going to be an asset to your race, real or chosen, or a liability.

I remember my dad giving me two teaspoons of Watkins Liniment in a glass of hot water and sugar for a cold. He roasted hogs hoofs on our potbelly stove and made hogs hooves tea for God knows what. Ginger tea stopped menstrual cramps. So did Red Pepper tea. We had Sassafras tea. Grandpa told me a story about Cow Manure tea. It seems this man had pneumonia and nothing the doctor did made him well. Before they introduced penicillin, people were dying in those days from pneumonia.

His family sent for a midwife who was equivalent to a naturalist with a little "roots" mixed in. This midwife told the man she could fix him up a little Cow Manure tea. He loudly refused. Each day he was getting worse. He sent for the midwife on the third day and asked her to fix this Cow Manure tea for him, and please give him a little manure to chew on while the tea was brewing. Needless to say, in Dad's story, the man got well.

There were remedies for worms in a kid's stomach. I had something called Nettle Rash Lumps about the size of half dollars all over my arms, legs, and thighs. Daddy would give me a large dose of Epsom salts in hot water and when my body finished eliminating this nasty, nasty medicine, the rash was also gone. Honest y'all! That's a family joke.

A cousin of mine on my stepfather's side, who came from a very strict religious family, was engaged to be married. She went to a hotel with her intended. They fell asleep and the next thing they knew it was morning. When they got home and tried to explain, they said they didn't have sex, they just talked. When they looked at the powers that be, they said, "Honest y'all"! That's been a family joke ever since; when an unbelievable needed to be believed.

Did you know flour water could stop diarrhea? I won't give you any proportions because I don't want you to try it; just giving you a glimpse at the "good old days". Baking soda, water and white vinegar was like Alka Seltzer. White vinegar was a good hair rinse. We used Vick's salve for colds; I think you call it Vapor Rub.

One reason I don't like goose meat is that it tastes like medicine. We took goose grease and also rubbed our chests with it. Sloans' Liniment was for aches and pains, Mutton Tallow for colds and rubs. A cough drop was made with a spoon of sugar and a little kerosene . . . burn it. Nine drops of turpentine in a spoon of sugar was for something. Soot from the stovepipe stopped the bleeding. Castor oil was suppose to bring on labor, if you were due. It didn't work.

They used to tell us there was a baby in every bottle of Lydia E. Pinkham and that Wine A Cardia was good for "women ailments". We gave children catnip for something. So you see, you guys are blessed to be here. I didn't use these cures on your parents, but suppose if my parents would have killed me with some of that stuff, you wouldn't be here.

I've also come full circle. My house is filled with health, vitamin, herb and nutrition books. I don't like treating symptoms. I like getting to the root and eliminating the problem. I eat garlic and take the tablets. My blood pressure and cholesterol is good. I drink all kinds of teas. I haven't gotten too much of the fresh herbs yet, but I make tea from my spice rack with sage, bay leaves, cinnamon, turmeric, ginger, cloves, etc. To make it interesting, I mix them. I use honey or sugar to sweeten and drink that instead of pop. It tastes good hot or cold.

Cola is another addiction on both sides of my family. Grandpa's oldest sister drank a pop every morning instead of having breakfast. She lived to be 98. Grandpa said she was older, but 98 is still a ripe old age.

It's so much easier for me to pray for someone else and have faith for them rather than to be in a situation and have faith for myself. Once I was on a plane in the Dallas Ft. Worth airport. The airport had to close due to a storm. We waited from 3 p.m. to 7 p.m. before we could take off. The airport was closed; nothing in and nothing out. After take-off, there was still turbulence. We went through beautiful sunshine to awesome darkness and all the weather in between. I prayed, quoted scriptures, sung under my breath and did a number of energy straining things. When I got home, my feet were twice their normal size. I got a good night's rest in my own bed. I woke up the next morning feeling fine and feet were back to normal.

Several of the children are going on a cruise this summer. It's going to be easy for me to believe God will give them a safe return. It won't take any energy and there will be no loss of sleep. I won't have to hear the winds, see the waves, or experience the turbulence and my feet won't be swollen. I don't need an adrenaline rush.

When I was younger, a gun was pointed at me in a robbery and that was exciting. A floor dropping beneath me in an amusement park and me sticking to a wall thrilled me. Helping to stop a riot and burning in the sixties was rewarding. Causing a rumble at the prison was exhilarating. Going one hundred twenty miles an hour in a car or riding a roller coaster was thrilling. Canoeing without a life jacket and not being able to swim or float when I was sixteen was daring. Now, what excites me is empowering, motivating, and helping others become the best person they can be. It excites me to meet a need if I can. It excites me to give people the love and attention they need and have missed. It excites me to lend a listening ear and a shoulder for someone to cry on as long as they get up and get on and leave space for a new person. So faith takes energy!

Emmit Till's wake, the young man in the Fifties who allegedly whistled at a white lady in Mississippi and was bludgeoned to death, was at Robert's Temple C.O.G.I.C. at 40th and State in Chicago. His body was there for several days. We drove from Chicago Heights to view the body. They didn't repair him; they left all the evidence of his beating. So many people were there; we couldn't get near the church. I suppose if we had waited long enough we could have, but after seeing his face in the "Jet Magazine" I wasn't too anxious to see him, so we left.

In 1957 our singing group went to Memphis to a convention. We went to a drive-in barbecue restaurant. We waited and waited. Finally a black man came out and told us we had to get out and come around to the back to be served. We declined. On the way back, our car had problems in Southern Illinois. We went into a restaurant. They told us they could fix us something to go, but we couldn't eat inside. We declined again. We went to a grocery store instead and bought enough to fix ourselves sandwiches. We went to the gas station and had to use the "colored toilet".

In Chicago Heights there were many places blacks couldn't go. I was in Washington Junior High School in 1949 and 1950. The Black students had to walk two blocks to get snacks. The restaurant next to the school didn't allow us to eat in there.

In those years I didn't know of any mixed churches. We had an Italian lady in our church, but she didn't appear to be accepted in the white community. Her sister was married to a black man.

A little white girl hollered, "Hello, you little black BB" as I was taking my dad his lunch one day. I was about eleven and she was about five. I jumped at her (instinctively) and she ran. When I got around the corner, I laughed until I cried. I know I wasn't what she called me, and I saw the humor in her inflection or term. Of course I couldn't let her see me laughing.

On Lowe Avenue we played hopscotch, roly poly, double dutch and hide and seek with the kids on my block: Lobu's, Piazza's Carducci's,

Amos', Damianio's, Hodges', Roop's, Rocha's and Lopez's. But we never went into their houses. Come to think of it, we played until their fathers came home. Most mothers stayed home. When we saw each other in school with their friends, I think we just ignored each other. Prejudice was alive and well in Chicago Heights in the 1950's. No Black people lived on the west side of Halsted. The railroad tracks and the downtown area separated the Blacks, the poor, and the Hispanics from the Whites.

I contend that if a woman sets her cap for you, in most cases she will get you. In my day we had a saying, "He chased me till I caught him"! We withheld sex and that kept our guys interested. Now your undisciplined lives are your downfall. I wouldn't want something easy. If it's easy for me to get, whom else is it being shared with? If a girl is beautiful and shapely, knows how to inflate your ego, listen to you wide-eyed and laugh at your jokes, nine times out of ten if you're not careful you will leave a happy home to find out that the grass isn't green at all and it isn't real grass. Use your head to think. Look at the big picture. Think of the ramifications. Suppose you get famous one day; who can come out of the woodwork and stake a claim? Keep out of dangerous situations. Someone can say you raped them if you're in a private place with no witnesses. If a woman is walking around naked, that doesn't give you a license to violate her. That's why we advocate celibacy until marriage. Grandpa Murphy said, "you loved them so much you could eat them, after you get them, you wish you had!"

Don't depend on the woman to use birth control. If you're not going to be celibate, be responsible and use a condom. No woman with any sense would accuse you of a baby if you haven't been there. If you have a baby, take care and make sure you include him or her in the family.

Marriage is beautiful. I had a policy that I would only date someone who was marriage material. When I found something in them that I couldn't live with, I'd quit them before I fell in love. Since love is a choice, I'd get out because had I continued dating them I would have chosen to fall in love with them in spite of the problem. I realize that I couldn't change anyone.

I used to make my boyfriends angry to see how they handled it. One hit the wall and busted his fist. I thought, "you wish that was me", so that was the end of that. The first nine years of my life was filled with fighting and I wasn't going to have it! So, my unsolicited advise to you is only to date a woman you would like to be the mother of your children, and at the proper time, marry her. This goes for the granddaughters also.

# CHAPTER FIFTEEN

I am more of a sporadic prayer person and not too much a public one. Talking to God is a private thing. I can think up pretty words to say to satisfy an audience, but I like to have intimate conversations. So when Sister Lang and I went on a shut-in for Barry, I said all I wanted to say and fell asleep. Every time I woke up, Sister Lang was praying. I'd say a little more and go back to sleep. We stayed three days and three nights. Every time I'd wake she was praying. I was amazed that she had so much to say. When I continue, it sounds like vain repetition. I don't know what else to say after I've confessed, praised, worshipped, and requested and given thanks.

I pray all through the day; while cooking, washing dishes, or taking a bath (my favorite time to pray). That's when I talk to my body and tell it to act right and give each organ some positive feedback. We had an old car that only responded to positive talking. When we started saying ugly things to it, it wouldn't budge. We'd say, "Come on baby, you can do it", "Good girl", etc., and she'd do it.

So after I've eaten correctly and exercised some, taken my vitamins, garlic and herbs, gotten the proper rest and have periodical check-ups (along with prayer), I encourage them to work properly. That's my kind of praying. I keep pictures over my sink in my kitchen so when I'm washing the dishes, I'm reminded to pray for those in the pictures. When I'm cooking, I pray for the people who are going to be eating the food. As I'm driving, I pray for the people on the roadways. So that's how I pray, two minutes here and five minutes there . . . sometimes in ten seconds, when a car pulls in front of me, or if a pit bull is coming my way. Seventy-two hours of uninterrupted prayer overwhelms me. Grandpa doesn't ask me to go on a shut-in with the church. He says my sleeping (I sleep loud) disturbs the prayers. That's okay by me. My bed sleeps much better than the church's floor.

Alex wouldn't let the kids do sports. Only Barton and Bretta were interested and good at it. Byron and Barry couldn't see the balls because they wore thick glasses. The doctor said they were almost legally blind. I had to think of something to keep them interested and occupied. I bought an upright piano for $25.00 in 1970. It cost more to move the piano than to purchase it.

From 1970 until now, they have always had access to a musical instrument. I went to the Salvation Army store and bought a guitar for Byron and a trumpet for Barry. At Christmastime I bought tambourines and other musical noisemakers so all of the kids could learn. Barry became a good trumpet player. He played until he started looking at girls. He didn't want his lips to look like Louis Armstrong so he put it down and took up the drums. He became very proficient on the drums then he became a firefighter and couldn't be faithful as the church's musician, so Barry, Jr., stood in for him. Barry is now practicing on the trumpet again. I know he will be good.

Barry wanted a girl. Mary likes to work. She was a city bus driver. They made a bargain; if she'd have a baby, he'd be a househusband and take care of the kids until the baby was in school all day; six years . . . to my dismay. That was unheard of in my day! My son, a pimp! I finally came to the conclusion that whatever a family decides to do; whatever makes them happy and lets them live harmoniously, if it works for them then so be it!

Barry liked his socks and his "pr yo" (pillow) like other babies love their blanket. He wore three or four pairs of socks at the same time. He would take a bath every day and put those socks back on until they were ready to fall off of him. I don't know if he had cold feet or not. Sometimes, before he graduated and started college, he changed that habit (I think). Barry is a firefighter and is back in school. He wants to be a lawyer.

I loved my first job. I like mastering a job so I work hard at learning; and when I was working I was thinking about how I could do a better job. I am friendly and I smile a lot so when they could, they would choose me. One lady got angry with me and asked, "Are you happy all the time"? Frankly, the majority of the time I am. When I'm not feeling up to par, I stay out of the way. I worked one year and three months at this supermarket. I never missed a day.

Aunt Flo charged me $5 a week. She would wash on Mondays, her day off work, and I would iron on Tuesdays, my day off. We kept the kids on our off days. She only had to pay a baby sitter for three days. Uncle Ezra kept them on his off day, Saturday. I was used to going to church every Sunday, but we might go every other Sunday at my new home. I loved this family and was taught a lot about family life and how to be a good wife and had a role model (or a good husband.

# CHAPTER SIXTEEN

There are certain rules I live by. Many of them are assumed which were given to me by my church or family. Some of them I formed and they are real. Some of the assumed values have become real to me:

- I must take a bath or shower daily; I do not leave my house without taking a bath.
- I wash my hands often, especially after using the toilet and handling money.
- Pray often.
- Read my Bible often.
- Go to church.
- Do not drink, smoke or do dope.
- Don't be an interfering mother-in-law.
- Keep confidences.
- Don't steal.
- Don't hold grudges.
- Eliminate troubles you don't have to have (you have enough that you can't eliminate).
- Don't divorce; and have a happy, peaceful home.
- Teach others what you know; and pick others' brains to learn from them.
- Read at least one book a month.
- Write letters to peoples' employers complimenting the employee when they have done an exceptional job.
- Be a giver of compliments, love and gifts, etc.
- Respect others' opinions, beliefs, traditions, culture and differences.

- Don't wear anything that hurts be it shoes or clothes.
- Don't watch X-rated or most R-rated movies.
- Never "front" your spouse in public. Talk to them in private.
- Be a good listener.
- Don't talk on the phone too long.

I have a theory; it might not be correct. I'm very opinionated and I know my opinion is not gospel all the time. I think our young people are watching these gory movies; watching people getting their head severed, being cut up, blood everywhere, etc. It's a way to program our youth whether it's on purpose or not, to accept murder or violence as a way of life.

Have you ever thought of things you have said you wouldn't do, then you find yourself doing it? I resisted the microwave as long as I could. I used to make cakes from scratch. One day someone bought me a boxed cake (cake mix). I tried it, using milk instead of water and melted butter instead of oil; a little more flavoring, and it was just as good as my scratch (and much cheaper)! Consequently, I very seldom make a homemade cake.

It won't be such a horror to see someone's head blown off, you see it everyday on TV, Blood used to be gruesome, but the movies are showing blood, mutilation, assassinations and how to do a perfect murder so much so that you kids think its normal. In 1941 mothers went to the war plants, fathers went to the Army and kids raised themselves. In 1961 (20 years later) hippies, yippies, gangs and free love. In 1981 (20 years later) the drug culture, STD's running rampant, abortions and teenage parents. Now in 2001 (20 years later) drive by shootings. It's up to you not to be in any of these statistics. It is your choice.

Many good things happened during this time also: technology, cures for many diseases, people left God and returned and opportunities galore. I have lived through all of this and have had more happy days than sad. I expect this to be the case until I die.

# CHAPTER SEVENTEEN

Grandpa was very sick in 1994. It was really hard for him being the pastor of a full gospel deliverance church. He preached the faith message. He believes in divine healing. He never tells the members to go to the doctor, and he never tells them to quit taking their medicine. When they get sick, they call for him to come and pray for them to improve.

I had not retired then, but was teaching coping skills in a vocational school. I also counseled in our church. I encouraged our students and parishioners to keep a positive attitude; to surround themselves with nutritious people and to read and view positive things. To look on the bright side, "Something good will come out of bad situations"! The bible says, "All things work together for the good to them that love the Lord and are called according to his purpose". I certainly love the Lord, so anything that happens to me must be working for my good. This theory was soon to be put to a serious test.

December 22, 1989, grandpa came home from his moonlighting lob (he worked for a car company to support the family, in case you forgot) and went to bed. He is a very active person, but I felt he was in bed because he needed the rest. He does work two jobs, was my rationale. He stayed in bed during all of the Christmas shopping and cooking. He got up for church that Sunday, but he didn't really feel like it. We were invited to some of the members' house for dinner on Christmas Eve. He only ate a piece of cake. I kept watching him. He hadn't drunk his favorite cola all week.

On Christmas Day, he was bedridden; just getting up to go to the bathroom. He only drank juices and water. I asked him if he wanted to go to the doctor, and he refused. On New Year's Eve we went to church and had our regular services without him. It is our tradition to be at church to welcome in the New Year. I tried to cancel the midnight service, but he wouldn't allow me to. He got out of bed and went on New Year's Day, which was Sunday. He preached one of his best sermons, but had to sit down to deliver it.

Afterwards we went out for breakfast. Coming home around 3 a.m. he entered a familiar curve, but lost control of the car. His equilibrium was off. We ended up in a field. If the ground had not been frozen, we would have been stuck in the mud. He was suppose to return to his job on January 2, 1990, but instead I took him to the doctor. The doctor said he had a bladder infection and gave him medication. We went home and promptly started him on the pills. He got somewhat better, but he was yet listless.

His birthday was Sunday, January seventh. Neither of us went to church. I had planned a surprise party for him. I cooked and bustled around the house unnoticed because he was too sick to care. He had forgotten it was his birthday. The people came at 5:30 p.m. He went downstairs to the party room, after much coercion. He could only stay one hour. The next day I got him dressed and took him back to the doctor.

They gave him more antibiotics because they found it wasn't a bladder infection, but a kidney infection. The pills that they had given him only made him sleep. He didn't know that he was in pain. On January 15th he couldn't go to church again. I kept telling your parents and the church that he was sick. We were taught not to claim sickness. By this time it had almost been a month. I didn't know any positive words to call his condition. I slept with him and heard his moans in the night.

When I asked him about the hospital he'd say, "No. I'll be all right". On January 16th some of your parents came over and prayed for him, which made him feel they were concerned. They noticed how hot he was as they touched him. About four o'clock that morning I happened to hear his groans in his sleep. I touched him and he was burning up with fever. I called 911. I got dressed and woke him up, put his robe on him and had him sitting up when the ambulance arrived. They asked him if he could walk to the cot. He couldn't remember the way out of our bedroom. He was almost delirious. When we arrived at the hospital, his temperature was 106 degrees. They took him in immediately and began treatment. They called his doctor. I asked them to give him a CAT Scan because, in my opinion, they had been hitting and missing with their diagnosis.

There is never a good time to be sick, and this was the worse possible time because the X-ray technicians were on strike. It took them almost six hours to service him. They found he had cysts on his kidneys. The infection had spread and was in his blood stream. They got the temperature down to 103 degrees, but it kept fluctuating. He was critical. We kept a twenty-four hour vigil. Grandma Gussie died with the same condition seven years earlier. Hers was complicated by diabetes. Also by the fact that the hospital and her doctor kept her in the hospital eleven days before they found out the real problem. They finally gave her a CAT Scan on the eleventh day and found an abscess around her kidneys. It was too late. The infection was too far-gone. Was history repeating itself? I wondered. "Oh God, don't let my husband die, I need him", I prayed.

Thursday, January 18th we almost lost him. We had to find a way to give him a will to live. I think he felt like a failure; that his members would not respect him any longer. How could he preach faith when he didn't have enough to be healed himself? My philosophy has always been, "Faith works"! My faith might not be up to par at this time, but it has nothing to do with God's power and his ability to heal. It's me, so I'll do what I have to do until my faith is built up again. I never experimented with your parents or you with faith, only on myself. So I would never experiment on Grandpa. I loved him and didn't want him to die. I did the next best thing. I took him to the hospital.

We are not a pill-taking family. We prayed about conditions. I gave the kids chicken soup, tea, juice, vitamins and love when they were ailing. Ninety percent of the time they got better. When they didn't in a day or so, I took them to the doctor. These were my thoughts as I was waiting by Grandpa's bedside. Wondering where I had gone wrong. It's easy to teach others not to feel guilty when things aren't going according to plans, but could I take my own counsel?

I had to rationalize with myself concerning Grandpa's illness. We have no qualms about going to an obstetrician, ophthalmologist, or dentist. Even some faith healers frequent these medical people. So why the double standard? That's almost like saying, "I'm an alcoholic. I can't drink beer, wine or whiskey, but I can drink vodka, gin and champagne". Chicken is chicken whatever fast food serves it.

I may sound like Job's wife in the Bible to some, but Grandpa is living and his sermons are so much more personal, laced with love and mercy of God. People are responding and we haven't heard one negative thing concerning his hospital stay. His strength, appetite, humor, vigor, and his fervor for the Bible had returned. Who knows whether he will submit to surgery when the doctors suggest it. It has been nine and a half years and he's healthy. They released him without surgery because he was too weak physically.

I have solved my problem. I trust God for complete healing for him one way or the other. Ideally a miracle, but I'll accept him whole even if the doctor has to do it. I love the old man. When this happened we had been married thirty one years. I have had more joy than sorrow, more peace than fury. I love him more today than I did December 5th, 1958. I don't want to lose him, especially for foolishness.

During this time, his best friend, Uncle Lawrence, died, who was also a minister. Alex heard about it on the answering machine. I had a deep conversation with him concerning his feelings about his own sickness and his friend's death. He had almost resigned himself to dying. Was it pride? Did he think God had let him down? Was he ashamed to face the congregation because he had lost his faith? I had to get him to talking about his feelings. I let him know that Iron wears out"! He was working two jobs, not eating properly, and drinking too may colas (my theory).

I tried to surround him with a pleasant atmosphere and laughter. I had planned to take a leave of absence from my job from January through March. He beat me to it. He wasn't able to go back to work until March. It's a standard joke with us that when I'm waiting on him to come home for dinner, I'll just fix my plate, sit at the table, take a first bite, and I'll hear his key in the door. He will come in hungry and ready to eat. He disrupted my leave just like he does my dinner many times.

Oh, he looked so helpless and so vulnerable. Here was this man who was strong and protective; who needed me to protect him. I teach setting priorities, how to deal with disappointments and decision making. Now was my time to apply and practice what I taught. Suddenly I realized I had power. The church would accept my decision. Your parents were just waiting for directions from me. Would I let religiosity get in my way? Would I be so heavenly minded that I would allow my husband to die? It's easy when you're looking at the news about someone else, and say what you'd do. When it's time for you to cross the bridge, it's another story. This was not my value. I have a low tolerance for pain so the few times my positive attitude, healthy habits and prayer didn't work, I went to the doctor. This didn't, and does not conflict with any of my values. It used to.

But to make a decision for someone else that is against their principles, caused me much concern. I have instructed your parents and now you not to let me linger on life support systems. Either God will heal me quickly or let the doctors give me something to make me comfortable so I can die peacefully. I had received no such instructions from my husband. Now that I have set precedence, I won't have to give it a second thought. We're going to pray and believe God for his health; and he gets regular checkups.

# CHAPTER EIGHTEEN

My sister Alice was sort of a misfit amongst all the dark-skinned people in Daddy's family. She took after her mother. She was very light skinned and had red hair. She really looked more like my mother's child than I did. Alice said Dad's side of the family mistreated her. She just didn't know that Aunt Leatha was mean. She treated me that way and I was dark.

Alice was mischievous like any regular kid. One day she was picking hot peppers from the garden. She didn't wash her hands before she went to the outhouse. Pepper somehow got in the wrong spot and she tore out of that place, and across the chicken yard, yelling for her sister Albertha. She jumped under the pump with her legs opened while Albertha pumped the water.

Alice was good to me when I was a teenager. She had seven children; three daughters and four sons. She taught herself to be one of the best beauticians in town. She could straighten and curl my hair and I'd have to wash the curls out. I didn't have to roll my hair and my hair didn't fall out. Her oldest two children were the first babies that I changed and washed diapers.

Alice and Albertha moved to Chicago Heights permanently when they were about fifteen and sixteen. Albertha worked and bought beautiful clothes; which I wore to school without her knowledge, until she caught me and put a quick stop to it. Albertha looked more like Daddy and his people than either of us did, but she had a kind and meek spirit. She never had any children. She married and moved to St. Louis and is still living there. Aunt Alice and five of her children are living here in Minneapolis. Those of you who come to church know several of them.

My Uncle Rufus Perkins, my mother's brother, had three children . . . Charles and Grace Perkins and Obadiah. When I was struggling with my small children, Charles used to visit me often. He knew I was having a hard time because my brother James had disappeared. Trying to comfort Miss Mary and keep my own family in order began to wear on me. Because Barry needed special care during this time and since I had to stay busy, I became a great cook. I loved feeding people, and I loved talking to Charles. That year I began gaining weight and couldn't stop.

I was not a stay-at-home person. Many things I didn't know; like you had to clean up all the time after children. I grew up an only child. I would get up at 6 a.m., fix Alex's breakfast and lunch, get him off to work by 6:30 a.m., and then have my quiet time until about 7:30 am. I'd read the Bible or some devotional book and pray. I would clean up the house and put on supper and cook breakfast.

We were on a schedule. I'd get up at 6 a.m. and the kids would wake up at 10 am. I had four hours to be with myself. Even though I was cooking and cleaning, it was therapy being busy and quiet. When the kids got up, we'd wash and eat breakfast. They would get dressed and try to clean their room. We'd have a busy day reading, singing, watching TV and playing. I would fix them lunch about 2 p.m. and we'd wind down because we all were going down for a nap when Alex got home. We slept from 3:30 to 5:30 p.m. every evening. Then we'd get up and eat supper together at the table. We'd clean up the kitchen (not Grandpa) then retire to the front room to watch TV.

The kids knew Aunt Alice, Cousin Charles, Grace and Uncle James. They didn't know Aunt Leatha. We moved to Minneapolis never knowing what happened to James. Miss Mary died about five years ago, never hearing from her only son again.

God is so good. When I was fifteen Miss Mary and my Dad adopted my Cousin Alfred's son who was also named Alfred. When Dad and Miss Mary separated, Alfred stayed with Miss Mary. We got him when he was thirteen months old. Miss Mary, being the loving person she was, brought him up to be a responsible person. Alfred was a teenager when James left.

At first we just thought James fell in love and left Chicago Heights to go to Chicago Proper or Detroit. There were plenty of rumors. After several years of not hearing from him, we sort of stopped our searching of jails, prisons, morgues, hospitals, etc. Alfred changed his name to James and took care of Miss Mary until she died. He took good care of her. She lived to see my children and Alfred's child. Every time we went to Chicago Heights, we went to see her. She was so proud to tell the people in her high-rise building that I was her daughter and these were her grandchildren. Miss Mary was such a great lady. She was a lady. She couldn't read or write, but she was very intelligent and had mother wit (common sense).

We yet have hope that we will hear from James. When people marry or have babies out of wedlock, you're not sure that last name your child could use. James could have used Byrd, Williams, Morris, or whatever Miss Mary's maiden name was. She was a Byrd when I met her, his father's name was Morris and my father's name was Williams.

# CHAPTER NINETEEN

My report card was never good enough unless I had all A's. My dad would say, "That's good, but it could have been an A". I graduated with three A's and a B. The B was in shop. He expected excellence from me, and I did my best to give it to him. He made me want to be the best at whatever I tried . . . be it daughter, wife, student, friend, employee, Christian, or whatever.

He asked me to light his cigarettes and I did until I was twelve and really got involved in my "smoking is sin church". In retrospect, our church was right in many aspects. No smoking, no drinking, celibacy before marriage, one marriage, and family values. Training, spanking, but not beating your children. Emphasizing education, testimonies, and you have what you say. It taught us public speaking and boldness. We never knew who would be called on to give the summary of the Bible lesson so we all studied. We couldn't compete in sports (we have since been enlightened), but we could compete in being the best Bible scholar, singer, musician, soul winner or best in education. Who would get their Bachelors, Masters, or PHD first. All things were not done to the glory of God, but we learned. The ones who sincerely loved the Lord didn't fall through the cracks. If someone did, they found their way home to God . . . if not to our denomination.

My dad was a no-nonsense person as a parent. You obeyed him without question. You knew he was in your corner. He got his bluff in on me at a young age. So after twelve, he never had to hit me; he punished me. Dr. Spock wasn't popular then, but Dad knew to take away something I liked if I displeased him. What liked was going to my church. He would make me go to his church for the next two or three months.

One day when I was thirteen, Dad threw me a dollar bill and said, "Here gal, go get you a brezer (bra). Dad knew very little about raising girls, but he was sincere. Once, we were making pyramids in gym; four girls were on the bottom, three girls on top of them, two more on top of them and then one on the very top. Well I was at the bottom. The next day I couldn't straighten up. The women told me that my body had fallen. On the third day I was a little better, but Dad gave me $5 to go to the doctor. A missionary was at our church carrying on a revival. At noon she was having prayer service. I went there instead of the doctor. She prayed for me and I got healed, so I gave her the $5. It seemed logical to me. Dad didn't ask me if I went to the doctor, he just saw that I was well. I didn't volunteer any information to Daddy. A lot of kids were sneaking off doing childish pranks etc., but I'd sneak off to do church things.

Dad was so strict. I could only listen to "Al Benson's Golden Gospel Hour, "The Wings Over Jordan" (a large spiritual choir from the south), and "The Grand Ole Opry"; no blues and no jazz. He wanted to protect my mind. When a girl my age got pregnant, I was not allowed to associate with her anymore. She was considered an adult. She could not continue school. Her education was finished. The girl was in "a family way" and the family was disgraced unless she got married. There were many "seven month babies", and it was explained to us teenagers that sometimes first babies came early. Now I know that many of them were already pregnant when they got married. That was the extent of our sex education.

Linda, a twenty-four year old who was 4'10" and ninety pounds, goes to our church. She has been a member since her early teens. Well, she got married to a 4'11" weight lifter. They make a beautiful couple. She got pregnant and at her delivery she wanted a lot of people there. She insisted on my being there. I think she and her family and the medical staff were very annoyed with me. I minister to the family when I go to the hospitals. I pick up all the pain of the patient. I will go in and let the sick person know that I'm there and then go to the waiting room and console and visit with the family.

Well, in Linda's mom I hollered every time she did. And as loud! That'll show them; no one else has ever asked me to hang out in their sick room. She has had two more children without inviting me.

Every year we had a garden at a community garden site and my dad (Murphy) taught me to set out plants and plant other seeds. I learned to weed and thin out plants. We got water from the nearby stream of water passing through this garden area. Later I learned that the reason the site was called the "Filthy Bed" was that water was sewer water. The veggies grew large and luscious.

# CHAPTER TWENTY

Bretta was born June 30, 1964. She weighed in at ten pounds and four ounces and was twenty-two and a half inches long. She had the fattest face I have ever seen. Her jaws hung down on her shoulders. Bretta had hair in the middle of her head and none in the front and none in the back. She came to the bed sucking those two fingers. I finally got my girl . . . my doll.

Carrying Bretta was different. She is the only one I lost a meal with. I caught measles while carrying her and had to have a gamma globulin shot. I went to prayer often with her. I wondered what the chances would be of having another ill child. I tried to do everything right, eating, exercising, prayer, etc. She came with only three hours and twenty minutes of labor. All of my babies, except Barry, slept all night when they got six weeks old.

Bretta was always in my space as she grew. All of the teenage girls loved her at the church in Chicago Heights, LaVerne and Linda especially. They would come and dress her and do her hair. I had no problem with getting a baby sitter, but I would just take the older girls with me so they could help me with the kids. I only left them alone when it was absolutely necessary.

When we moved to Minneapolis in 1967, Bretta began having problems. Her little girlfriends would come to see her because they liked her brothers. Her dearest friend Janice liked Barry. All through the years she didn't know whether the girls were befriending her to get next to her brothers or because they liked her. Bretta sort of felt inferior to the guys. Bart played drums, sax and guitar. Mike played congas. Barry played trumpet and drums. Byron played guitar, drums and keyboards. Bretta wasn't musically inclined that way. She had a voice. She joined many choirs as she grew older and learned a lot of things from her directors. She has had many directors who are popular now. She has an alto voice, but she can give all three parts. So, for years now, she has directed our choir and is doing a fantastic job. I don't think she has any professional singers; just folk who are willing to learn and I can see them growing together. They have given two concerts at the Women's Correctional Facility in Shakopee, Minnesota, and have gone to Omaha and Chicago. So, every year they have done at least one major thing. She has finally found her niche. She takes many classes. She graduated from one vocational school, one secretarial school, Dale Carnegie Course, and is enrolled at Metro State College. With her determination, she will finish college.

Remember I told you that Aunt Bretta stayed in my space? Well, I had a very good male acquaintance. He was too young to be a friend and too old to be a son. I counseled him concerning two women. I knew his strengths and weaknesses. Well, Bretta fell in love with him. I didn't approve because I knew his philosophy concerning love and marriage. She was twenty and grown. All I could do was pray. One day her values were challenged: she got over him. She is 6'1" and I'm 5'4". I don't remember curling her up in my arms and rocking her. I wished I could have taken her pain.

Well, in 1986, Uncle Cecil came into her life. They got engaged. The church gave us a twenty-eight year wedding-vow-renewal with a sit-down dinner. Bretta and Cecil had gotten their license and decided that day to horn in on our wedding. We had a double wedding. Many of you grand kids were there, the ones fourteen and over. Bretta wasn't dressed for a wedding but Debbie Bell, my daughter-in-law, had on a pretty yellow dress and hat. She traded with Bretta and we had a great wedding. Uncle Cecil is good for Bretta. He is about a head shorter, but the guy that broke her heart was four or five inches taller. Height doesn't make a man right for you.

They were married four years before she got pregnant. She had a hard delivery so she tells us that Ebony is the only baby coming through her body. She is the only one who I wished had another baby. Ebony is to Bretta as Bretta was to me . . . in her space! She was even born on Bretta's birthday.

Auntie Bretta is my dear one, and she is secure in my love. She has no problem with me being close to my daughters-in-law and my adopted daughters. All of her friends call me Mom, but she says, "I know I'm your only real daughter". Women grow tall on Grandpa Alex's side of the family. Aunt Birdie is 6', Natalie and Paula are one inch shorter and one inch taller than Bretta.

Your parents were as enamored with my mother as I was with my grandmother. So when Grandma Gussie died, we had to take at least a year to recover. It didn't occur to me to put the kids in therapy or at least in a grief clinic. I had survived my grandmother's death and was struggling to survive my mother's. I thought just family togetherness would heal the wounds. The guys got into some negative behavior that took time and prayer to get them out of. Bretta surrounded herself with choirs and friends.

# CHAPTER TWENTY ONE

On or about August 15th, 1965, Byron was conceived. By October 30th I started having trouble with him. He was the busiest baby I had carried. He loved swimming, stretching and tumbling. You might think he was too young to start that, but "honest y'all" I thought he was twins. From November till he was born, April 28, 1966, he asserted his individuality, "Don't fence me in, I'll show you"! He loved to lie on the left side of my stomach. Then he'd stretch and press against my heart and bladder (that's what it felt like). I couldn't sleep lying down from the seventh month till after delivery. I had to sleep sitting up in an overstuffed sofa chair (ottoman).

He was a prankster even then. At delivery time the doctor would say I was ready and then they'd say, "Oops, he's gone swimming"! I was taken to the delivery room three times and three times he "went swimming". When he decided to come, there was no available delivery room for me. I wanted to give him a good spanking as my first official act to him. He weighed in at ten pounds and two ounces. When they brought Byron to me for feeding, he was so sweet. How could this be the same baby that had given me so much heck when I was carrying him?

I soon found out he was one and the same. He nursed my left breast, but would go to sleep when I'd turn him and give him my right one. I had to have my right breast pumped because he refused it. I couldn't let a baby out-smart me; after all I was the parent! I thought about his erratic behavior in the womb and decided he didn't like to lie on his right side. I thought I would fool him and keep him on the side he likes and push him under my arm to see if he would nurse. He did! So that's how I fed him and made myself comfortable because he emptied both breasts. When Byron decided to, he ate the right way.

The other kids sucked the ring and index lingers. Byron sucked his thumb. I don't remember back packs for babies in those days, but I had to cook with him on my hip. He wanted and needed much attention. It was good we had a lot of family around. When he was old enough to stand up and look out of the window, he became fascinated with police cars, fire trucks and ambulance sirens and lights. Upon hearing the sirens, he would pull himself up to the window and peer until he'd see the lights then he'd holler, "light, light". He was fascinated, but also scared by them.

I bought Byron a guitar from the Salvation Army Store for $5 (1971) without any strings. We fixed it up and Byron would lay it across his lap and play it. He took it to kindergarten for show and tell. That's when I knew he had musical talent.

Byron and Teresa have five children; four sons and one daughter. Byron was our keyboardist until another one came. Now he mostly does praise service. He is an ordained Elder. He has a class called "Dedicated to Excellence" and Teresa has a class called "Women Dedicated to Excellence". Uncle Byron still annoys me. He is so nosy when it comes to me, "Where are you going, who with, who are you talking to, who is that letter from", etc. He is never disrespectful. In fact, if he is "cuttin up" in church I can still snap my fingers and he will snap to attention. Then he remembers he's grown, but he will stop his misbehaving.

We have a friend who is blind. Byron has been pushing her buttons ever since he was a teenager. I think Julie would think he was neglecting her if he didn't meddle her one time. Whenever she needs someone to take her shopping, she would call Byron and Teresa. She knows they love her.

Byron is the nosiest person I know. When he was about five I found a tampon with b.m. (bowel movement) on it in the garbage can. Evidently he had been peeping when I had been in the bathroom (remember Mary, Herbert and I had a peephole on Lowe Avenue?), doing my private things. He knew it went somewhere and didn't have but one cavity so he tried to use that one. It must have hurt so he discarded it. Before that he had put a sanitary napkin on our cat. The adhesive stuck to the fur.

One cold Minnesota day, he got his tongue stuck to the metal hand railing on the walk in the yard. I didn't know what to do but get some warm water and pour it on his tongue and rail. It worked. We lived in a duplex when Byron was three years old. The father of the family who lived upstairs was a prolific cursor. Byron used to sit on the steps in the hall and listen and learn these words. It took many years for him to break that habit. He didn't let us hear him, but the children found ways of letting us know.

One day after we had moved to a one-dwelling house where the bedrooms were upstairs, Byron found his favorite spot by the window on the landing halfway up the stairs. He would stand there and holler at the kids coming home from school. He told them that his brothers and sister were going to whip their a_ _ _ _. These kids would be waiting on Bart, Barry and Bretta when they got near the alley in the back of our house. Byron's mouth had gotten them in trouble again.

So Bad thought of a good pay back for Byron. Alex taped his Bible studies to play back at his young people's class (YPWW) on Sunday nights. One Sunday night we heard some voices on the tape. Bart was daring Byron to "not say that word", and "I dare you to say that word Byron". And, after a few dares, a high-pitched voice said, "S_ _ _. There, I've said it"!!! Well, the entire Bible class heard it. Alex said, "What's this, what's this", and played it again. Oh Bible study was over!

Teresa, Taj, Tiffany, Byron Jr., and Blayr put up with him. I can't even imagine how they do it. Sometimes I ask him, "Who died and left you boss"? He checks up on me more than my husband does. They have been good for each other.

One day during his grieving for my mother, he and Milton went to the State Fair and met two girls. Troy was born of that union. He took a DNA last year and found him to be his son and has been paying child support ever since. When you have missed thirteen years in a child's life, it's hard to catch up, but not impossible. He is just as much a grandchild as any of the others.

A letter to me from Teresa: "Dearest Mom, I don't think I've written you a letter before, and I should have. After watching "Soul Food" last night, I was urged to write you even as I watched the movie. I just want you to know that you are the 'Big Mama' in my life as she was to her family. I am so grateful for so many traits that you have. I have forgotten along the way that one of my greatest gifts is honesty from the heart, so I need to exercise it more. You have been more to me, and continue to be, the mom I've always wanted but have been cheated from since childhood . . . taking nothing from the fact that I have a mother, only adding to the fact that you've given me and showed me what is needed to make it through the rest of this life, successfully. I didn't know much about womanhood, motherhood, or wifehood. Yet you continue to teach me so much. You,

Dad, and Byron have a piece of my head that I wouldn't give to anyone else. It's not just the financial help, although it is a great part, but it is the learning process, the scrutiny that imbeds my soul—it has changed me; it has taught me; it is essential for me to learn from you for I know not another I'd want to learn from. You are so many things to me that you know not how valuable you are and have been. I thank Almighty God for searching the world for the family that I had need of—the man and woman of God who would be the most influential people in my life besides my husband. I've seen how there have been times that you "caught flack" for putting together "outings" and such, only to have a glorious outcome. I'm learning. I see you outstretch your arms to those who I've thought unworthy. I'm learning. I watch you carry on when carrying on was almost unthinkable. I'm learning. I've watched your wisdom come through teaching, counseling, preaching, meetings, etc. I'm learning. I've heard the Word come out of you so natural. I'm learning. I see you give, and give, and give. I'm learning. I see your love that hasn't said, "I told you so". I'm learning. No, I'm not putting you on a pedestal, because we both know it's really God when it all comes down to it, but I am saying you are all I'd ever want to be, and more. I want the compassion/love that keeps <u>you</u> going. When I watch you I know I'm far from being there but through the ever-learning process I know I'll some day make it too. I just want to thank you for all the times you've expended yourself <u>without complaining</u>, and all the times you've been there for "ME". My life has changed since I met you. My ministry, my marriage, my future, my past is changed because I know you. Just so that you don't get scared . . . Truly Christ is my all in all! So, in closing, I may come across as a know-it-alt, it's really just my insecurity. I want to thank you for your investment into my life—the payoff (spiritually/financially) will all have been worth it. Thank you Mom, P.S. This letter requires no response. Please accept my appreciativeness! Teresa"

# CHAPTER TWENTY TWO

Michael was born April 28, 1952. I was fifteen going on sixteen. I was not allowed to be talking to Alex. When my dad found out Alex had fathered a child, he sat me down and told me if he would do that to Michael's mother he would do it to me; get me pregnant and not marry her. He promised to shoot us on sight if he saw us as much as talking.

I spent the summer of 1952 in Chicago with Mother and Mr. Willie. When I returned, Michael was four months old and living with Alex's older sister, Aunt Emma. Aunt Emma and Mike moved to Pembroke, Kentucky, when he was about four years old. Alex still hadn't married. I left town for one year and three months from June 1954 till September 1955. I stayed home about six months and left again. I wanted to make sure I was not the cause of Alex not marrying his son's mother.

Michael was the apple of Aunt Emma's eye. He was a beautiful, well-mannered child. He was sent to Sunday school every Sunday. Mike has the most beautiful smile and teeth than all the kids. After Alex and I married, Aunt Emma wanted to see if he would stay with us. I helped him with his math, but he would only stay two or three days. He was an only child at Aunt Emma's and he had to share us with three kids. He wasn't having it.

When he and Sis (as we called Aunt Emma), moved to Kentucky I called and asked her to send me some Red Clay dirt. I was craving it with one of the pregnancies. Mike went out and dug me a bag. When I got it, I put the dirt in some water. I strained out the rocks and baked the water out of it. Whenever I ate, I got a taste for this dirt. I'd eat a little piece and be satisfied. Later I learned that my body was craving whatever minerals that was in the dirt.

Mike and Sis came back to Chicago Heights when he was about ten. He was sent to Minnesota in 1968. He finished school here in Minneapolis and enlisted in the Navy. He looked so good in his uniform.

When he was discharged, he came back to Minneapolis and met Linda and eventually got married. When they were expecting their first child, I told Linda I didn't know if I was ready to be a grandmother. Her answer was, "Ready or not, here he comes"! Linda and I became friends. She is such a great help to me at the church. She has a degree in Nutrition. I'm a good cook, but I do it by instinct. You know . . . a pinch of this and a pinch of that. But she knows the how's and why's. We make a good team. They have given me three wonderful grandchildren: Jason, Michael Jr., and Avalyn.

Michael graduated as a Computer Technician and is an accomplished conga player in the church's band. He also has a beautiful tenor voice. Michael is so funny. One day he called us from downstairs (Marquette address) and told us he had a way to build the church and a way we could get all we needed. He was so excited and very, very serious. When we found out it was one of the get-rich-quick schemes, I'm sure we busted his bubble. He was undaunted. He carried on until he was convinced it wasn't going to work for him. Michael has a mind of his own. He was born on the same day as his youngest brother; just thirteen years earlier. He and Byron are similar—they are both left handed.

# CHAPTER TWENTY THREE

I met Judi in 1973. I was working at Minneapolis Urban League on a special project. This young lady came in from lunch and she reminded me of Cher. She already had Matt, a beautiful baby boy. Nicky (Shalom), Ashabi and Ramesa came later. They were beautiful and I rocked them all to sleep. Since they are all still living, I will only say that Judi made an impact on me. She typed the church's first newsletter. She was on our prison team and was there when the church first started. She went from my spiritual baby to my daughter to my friend.

She moved back home to Mount Vernon and I miss her very much, but I knew she had to go. Nicky came back to finish school. She was the first grandchild to stay with us without a parent. She wasn't a rebellious teen. We had rules and she adhered to them. We have a lot in common. She loves to read also and she was my running buddy. We could go to plays together.

We visited Judi and the kids three times in the years they've been gone. Ashabi came and spent a week or two one summer; and I think they all came once. Distance makes your phone bills high and you can't be too lazy about writing; otherwise you lose touch and that isn't good for families.

There was a lady in the church who was in love with Grandpa in 1978. Judi, Diane and Pat offered to beat her up for me. I told the lady that love was never wrong—lust is wrong. That is, if she Indeed loved my husband she would not try to corner him at every opportunity. She would want to enhance his reputation, not damage it. It doesn't matter to me who loves my husband it matters to me who my husband loves.

# CHAPTER TWENTY FOUR

How well do you know me? I used to give a test to my class starting about ten years ago asking how well do you know your loved ones. There will be some things you might not learn from this letter, so I'll tell you.

My favorite color used to be yellow, now it's blue—all hues.

My favorite music is Gospel. I also like Jazz and whatever kind Lou Rawls sings, and some Blues. I like words I can understand and instrumentals. Look up some old Earl Garner's music. I've used Bobby Blue Bland's "I'll Take Care of You" for my self-esteem class. I tell people to say that to themselves, and do it. Also "One In a Million", and "You'll Never Find" were great!

I bought "A Phone Call from God" when the kids were teens. It was Country & Western. We would listen to that almost every day. Even now after about twenty years, I can ask one of the kids what did the preacher preach on and they will say, "On a platform" and we all begin to laugh. We lost, or loaned, that cassette tape and can't find it because we don't know who the artist is. "Attitude Adjustment" was another good one.

One day as we were driving to Seattle, we drove into a storm on one of those mountains in Idaho or Montana. The lightening was striking the trees and some of them were catching on fire. It was midday, but it was as dark as midnight. Thunder was loud and it was raining. I can't remember being as scared; except maybe when my neighbor died when I was a kid. I reached in the glove compartment and found Vanessa Bell Armstrong's "Peace Be Still" and as it started playing, all fear left me. I played that song until we were out of danger.

There's one rap I used to use in my class. I had each person bring in their favorite song on tape. I called it music therapy. We listened to all the tapes, with all types of music, and discussed how we felt while listening and what we felt like doing. Some music was to dine by, or do housework to, or exercise by, etc. I told them I would bring the rap. It was "Hear the Word". It was a fantastic Bible rap. I could understand every word.

The book that has had the greatest impact on me was In His Steps by Charles M. Sheldon. I read it when I was in high school (I think). I like all kinds of books. I tend to fall in love with authors. If I read a book and like it, I try to read all that author's books. Pearl S. Buck took me to China many times. John Grisham took me to court and other interesting places. Eugenia Price, Taylor Caldwell and many, many others entertained me. The Godfather was great and The Final Diagnosis made me have more faith in God. It was about a bungling pathologist.

My favorite TV programs were/are, "Beverly Hillbillies", "Highway to Heaven", "Touched by an Angel", and most comedies. Norman Cousins said he laughed his way back to health, so I feel I can stay healthy by laughing. The Bible says that laughter is medicine.

I will go out of my way to drive through the parkways to see rabbits and other critters. I love to see animals in their habitat. My favorite animals are deer, ducks and rabbits. Oh yes, I read the Watership Down, one of my favorite. I don't eat those animals either (rabbits).

# CHAPTER TWENTY FIVE

Some other rules I live by that I'd like to shale with you:

- Have good health practices
- Unless you have faith that your spouse's hand will wither in mid air, get you and your children out of an abusive relationship and then pray for the person to change.
- Put more money in the parking meter than you think you'll need, just in case.
- Send a thank you letter to people who help. Don't be a "slop eater", only looking up when the slop stops!
- Flush the toilet after each use.
- If you are sharing a bathroom with the opposite sex, don't argue if the seat is left up; he has just as much right to complain if the seat is left down . . . it's his house too!
- Pick up after yourself unless you have money to pay for a maid.
- Be courteous to your waitperson. If you can't out of courtesy, then do it out of fear. They could do unkind things to your food.
- Be kind to the janitor or secretary. They can make you look good or bad. The janitor can make you very uncomfortable; hot in the summer and cold in the winter. Your office or space may seldom get cleaned, and just enough so you would sound petty if you complained. It you need things moved or supplies, the janitor can set priorities so that your request is low priority.
- Regulate what goes into your mind and body.
- Assess your day. Fix the things you can fix; grieve over the things you can fix (for about ten minutes) then RECOVER and move on.

- Bathe daily (preferably a whole bath) or at least sponging all the vital parts.
- Brush your teeth at least twice a day and carry breath mints.
- If offered a breath mint, don't refuse it, you might need it! The person could be trying to tell you something.
- Get a cavity filled before you lose the whole tooth.
- If you don't brush after lunch, at least rinse your mouth out. You might go to your next meeting with food between your teeth.
- Check your nose several times a day to see if boogers are showing.
- Speak to and identify yourself with the person who answers the phone; especially if you are asking for their mate.
- Keep your animals in another room when you have company. Everyone doesn't like them. Some are afraid of them and many are allergic to them. Some people just detest animals rubbing against their legs or jumping on them. And they (cats) will usually show guests that you allow them to jump on countertops, etc.
- Let all of your doctors know what other medicines you are taking.
- Get as much education or training you can get so you won't have to depend on anyone.
- Since you are growing older, do it graciously and with dignity. Lighten up your hair. Cut down on the make-up, and lower your skirts by at least 75!
- Realize that several days without prayer will make you anemic.
- Fasten your seat belts.
- Watch out for cars, no matter what color the light is.
- Never go against the light, especially when you are with children. You are training them to disobey safety laws.
- Surprise your children at school (K through 12). Start a new tradition; PARENTS MAY POP UP AT ANYTIME . . . out of concern.
- Pick "junk" up off the floor; don't keep stepping over it.
- Take the garbage out before it starts stinking. Put it in a secure container so animals won't strew it.
- Write appointments down and frequently check your appointment book.

- Look at the elevator to see if it's going the way you want to go. Make sure you are getting off on the right floor.
- Don't get on an elevator with people who make you feel unsafe.
- Travel in pairs at night if possible.
- Lock your doors, house, car and windows.
- Pull your shades down when dressing.
- Since this is the only body that you are going to have in this would, take good care of it
- Wear shoes in your house so that you won't break your toe on a chair or table leg (experience).
- It you have a bladder problem, don't sit in the front of the church. No one wants to buy a videotape advertising your bathroom treks.
- IT'S A THIN LINE BETWEEN COMMON SENSE AND COMMON COURTESY.
- Start buying or making your yearly gifts at the beginning of the year. Things made by you are much more meaningful. Start a tradition . . . Grandma isn't buying or giving money, she is making mine.
- Hang up on a prank, abusive, or any negative phone call. You pay the bill, or at least this is your phone.

# CHAPTER TWENTY SIX

How To Stay Married Till Death Do You Part:

1. If your spouse can put up with you and your faults, you should return the favor.
2. If you love a clean kitchen and your mate loves clean clothes, you clean the kitchen and let them do the wash.
3. Clean up behind yourself.
4. Don't require that the other person do the chore like you do it; just as long as it gets done.
5. Whoever handles the money best should handle it.
6. Budget, but leave a little to splurge on every now and then.
7. Take mini family vacations. We used to fill the car up and choose a highway at random then drive until the car was half full and start back home. Once it was too late to start back home (we were in Alexandria, Minnesota). We got a motel and stayed the night. The kids had fun on the vibrating bed!
8. Respect each other.
9. Communicate.
10. Don't go into marriage looking out. Think "stay, stay" not "go, go".
11. Since marriage is a business and every member of the family owns stock in this business, it's to everyone's advantage to protect their investment. Everyone loses when there's a separation and merger of different families.
12. Be faithful and trustworthy.
13. Keep yourself up.

14. Don't become common with each other. Wash your own underpants. She won't see the skid marks and he won't see the menstrual leaks.
15. Forgive and forget.
16. Don't nag, fuss or whine.
17. Share the load.
18. Be comforting.
19. Be a friend, lover, parent as well as a spouse.
20. Give each other space.
21. Don't be suspicious of everyone they talk to.
22. Be fun to live with.
23. Make home so pleasant that your spouse can't wait to get there.
24. Don't tell family secrets. Some things should be between you and your mate.
25. Have a family night.
26. Go to your religious establishment together.
27. Do a sport together; golf, bowling, swimming, jogging, walking or exercising, etc.
28. Read the newspaper or watch the news so that you can have something to talk about other than family problems.
29. Be unpredictable.
30. When life begins to wear you out, encourage them to get some teeth, lose weight, get a new hairdo or color, etc. Anything to make them feel good about themselves. (I bought Grandpa two pair of partial plates. He lost one pair and sent the other pair to the cleaners. So I let him go "snaggletooth" for a few years. He clearly didn't want them. Grandpa loves to "grin"; he doesn't just smile. One day a dentist met him at a wedding of a mutual friend. Grandpa did the inspirational message before the vows. The Lord put it on the dentist's heart to fix Grandpa's teeth. After a few conversations, they got together. His teeth were beautiful. We went to Detroit to visit grand kids. He hadn't gotten use to eating with them in his mouth. He look them out and accidentally left them at the restaurant. Doctor checked on Grandpa. He had to admit he had lost the pair of teeth. So he graciously fitted him with another pair. We let our insurance pay as much as they would and he donated the rest. We went to Detroit again and were on our way to the airport to come home when I asked him if he had

his teeth. He did not. We turned around and the maid was just cleaning our room. She had his teeth in a glass on her cart. Doctor comes periodically to Grandpa's Bible class. One evening he came and no teeth! So Grandpa tries not to forget them because he never knows when the doctor will pop in to see his work of art. I permed my hair for many years. After I got out of the natural, I went to the curl and then a straight perm. It took a toll on my hair. I decided to never perm my hair again. I have kept to that for six years. I stayed in braids for two years. I'm lazy when it comes to my hair. I used to go to the beauty shop every week. I tried to keep it natural, and it was so much work that I bought a wig. It was almost as easy as the braids. I bought another one, then another one and so on. I have about seven wigs, all different lengths and colors. Grandpa doesn't mind and the church thinks it's hilarious. I'm not trying to pretend it's my hair, but it is because I paid for it. They never know what I will look like. But ninety five percent of the time, they like what they see. My point is; look good to yourself and to your mate.

31. Grow. Try to grow together, not necessarily in the same area. Just don't become stagnant so that you'll stay interesting to each other.

32. Keep a scrapbook, album, or date book to remember good times in the trying times.

33. Repeat family stories. The Bible says to rehearse it so they won't forget it.

34. Do something special during the holidays that you can keep up every year; something that your children will remember. I remember the box by my bed on Christmas Eve night. My father told me that Santa Clause would put ashes in my eyes if I saw him. So I slept, or pretended I was asleep. I would get up on Christmas morning with things in my box; fruit, clothes and maybe a toy or two. I don't know when I realized that Dad was my Santa Claus; probably when I found out that rabbits didn't bring babies. I never taught you about Santa Clause or the tooth fairy. I did put the box by your bed and put money under your pillow if you put a tooth under it. I would tell you guys to try and catch the person who placed them there. It was always a game with us—to catch the benefactor. We used to have a tradition of having pizza

every Friday night. Now when your parents come to the house on Friday nights they expect pizza.

35. Go on a long trip together. Something they can remember for years to come. We went to Dallas. Texas. They loved staying in the motels and eating out.

36. Have friends who have children so they can visit while you visit, and you know they share similar values.

37. Go on a date like you use to.

38. Be independently dependent on each other. Let the person know you need them, but don't be desperate. I learned to drive because I was tired of waiting on Grandpa to decide to take me somewhere. I actually learned by doing. I got there and back safely the first time and every Saturday I drove until I became proficient at it. I love to be chauffeured and a lot of people don't know I can drive. But I learned so I can be independent. If someone wants to drive me it's great. But it's not because I can't.

# CHAPTER TWENTY SEVEN

Aunt Jessie was my father's (Murphy) and Aunt Leatha's sister. She was the youngest sibling. She had three sons—Eddie, Charles and Elbert. She and my mother were friends. In fact, she was with my mother when Daddy shot over their head and Aunt Rosie got up and ran, after being paralyzed for many years. Daddy sent for Aunt Jessie and her kids after he married Miss Mary. She lived next door to us. She was much more pleasant than Aunt Leatha was. When I ran away from your grandfather I went to Chicago Heights to be with my dad, but I slept at Aunt Jessie's house. About twenty years after that, I got a call from my stepmother, Queenie, saying Aunt Jessie was critically ill. I flew in and checked into the hotel, took a taxi to the hospital in Harvey and met my cousin Lilly and a few others there. Aunt Jessie was in a coma.

When they left the room, I did something I had read about. I read a lot and if something intrigues me, I try it. I had read and heard that comatose people can hear you. So I began talking to Aunt Jessie softly, near her ear. I told her I loved her and talked about pleasant things in the past, some funny things like Daddy and the shooting. I told her that she could die if she wanted to; it was her choice. I asked her if she was ready to meet her Maker. If she had forgiven everyone, and had she asked for forgiveness. I rattled on and on. The family let me stay in her room alone because they had been keeping the vigil for almost a week.

After I had talked out, I began to pray. I told her that since she was a believer, and so was I, that if she wanted to get better she could agree with me and God would heal her. All of a sudden her eyes popped open and stared at me. My heart almost jumped out of my chest. If I had had to go to the bathroom, then I would have went number one, two and three! I know the Bible says I have the power to tread on serpents and raise the

120

dead; but let me raise the spiritual, emotional and financially dead, not the physical! I quickly called the nurse. It was almost like me calling U. S. West to get my Internet connected. I am computer illiterate. Once I'm put in a program, I can type, spell-check and save, etc., but that's about all. The operator asked me if I had a modem. Well, I didn't know what a modem was so I told her I'd get back to her and hung up the phone. I felt the same way when Aunt Jessie's eyes opened. Especially when she fixed them on me. In essence, I told God, "I'll get back to you", and quickly left the room. I slept with the lights on at the hotel that night. Aunt Jessie went home and lived approximately six months, then died suddenly of a heart attack. Alex, Uncle Byron and I went to the funeral and she looked like an older me lying in that coffin.

I am fast approaching the eldest in my family. None of them have given me much history. That's why I have to start from where I know Simon Perkins and Mary Range. Seeing Aunt Jessie dead made me realize that I needed to let my grandchildren know where they get their health problems and their inherited traits. Most of my boyfriends had beautiful noses (in my opinion). My nose is short and pudgy. I wanted my children to get Alex's nose—a little longer and more pointed. All of our kids have my nose and it has been passed down to most of our grand kids. As you read this legacy, you will find yourselves in here many times.

I have tiled to say "the buck stops here" where marriage and alcohol are concerned. You can make a marriage work, you can have all of your children by one person, and if you never take the first drink, you will never become an alcoholic.

# CHAPTER TWENTY EIGHT

A Letter To My Grandchild:

I think it's about time we talked. I started to wake you up this morning when I got up at six a.m., but I wanted you to have your weekend.

I think our expectations are different. So I will tell you what I thought yours were and I will tell you what mine are. I will also tell you my idiosyncrasies. The things that make me act an idiot, or sin, or drive me crazy.

I thought your expectations were to be in a safe, loving home where you could relax, serve the Lord and be in the cities with friends and family. I think we have met that expectation. You must tell us if we have disappointed you and if there were more than I have named.

This morning (Sunday) I got up and the food was yet on the stove. Everything was just as I left it when I went to bed at 10:30 last night. If you had been observant of me, you would know that going to bed that early with my kitchen looking like that is out of character for me. I don't like to complain. I have told you before that when I'm in the bed more than usual and when my kitchen isn't clean, I'm not feeling my best.

I thought this morning at least the food would have been put up and the dishwasher at least unloaded. You know I have all these greens to wash for the party. I have to cook all this week: two turkeys, two roasts, fifteen pounds of potato salad, and on and on. I yet have more shopping to do.

Because I love you, I try to do things to make you happy. Sometimes you don't have to ask me. I see the need and try to meet it. I refused to be used. When I feel like I'm the one doing all the loving and giving and someone else is just receiving, I will go on strike. Ask the kids. I didn't cook or clean, but came home just to sleep and let everyone fend for themselves. Finally they got the message.

Take an inventory. List the things you have done this week. There are things I can't do like mop, vacuum and sweep. The twisting and bending hurt my joints. If you notice me when I get up, I'm hobbling. I need help up and down stairs. But I do what I can do—cook. I even clean the toilet bowls; Dad's and ours. I don't ask people to do unpleasant things like cleaning the toilets. But sweeping the toilet floor, putting stuff in place, cleaning up after yourself, emptying the dishwasher and other things that's needed to be done I would appreciate.

This is our house. I am embarrassed when someone comes and the house isn't clean. I don't mean perfect, but clothes hung up, garbage not overflowing, no cans laying around, etc. I would think you'd be too, because this is where you live. I told you when you first came that I'd like to keep the front room and table, kitchen and front bathroom clean, also the hall presentable for when company comes.

Last weekend you had PMS so I let you sleep until almost choir rehearsal time (two o'clock). This Saturday you got up and by the time you could straighten up, Milton was here and it wasn't much we could do. Last night you read your books and did things for you, but I can't see anything you did for the house.

Grandpa and I are really generous. That's because we are givers. I know sometimes you hate getting his ice or water or doing things for him, but it's probably because you aren't use to it. I just want you to think of the exchange. There are no free lunches. People pay for whatever they get. Some people pay in time. I pay for my keep by having meals ready, shopping and having food in the house, keeping the utilities on and the other bills paid. I counsel the members so Grandpa can have a clear mind to preach. I go to the hospitals and the courts with the members and their children. I take care of the women and the Sunday school plus I try to do the things that God has given me to do, which is write. I have to read so I can write. When I'm doing these things, it's my job. I'm not doing it just because I want to. Many times I'm not even enjoying it. I have to do it.

My family should make it as easy for me as I make it for them. I hate arguing. I think an intelligent person shouldn't have to be told every little thing to do. Why step over a piece of paper; pick it up. If you were just a roomer, we could have assigned jobs; but you are a part of this family and we are in this together. Grandpa and I have worked since we were teenagers. We are retired now, but we work harder with the church than we did on our jobs.

You need a job, vitamins, and a purpose in life. You are young and I am sixty-one and a half. I have more energy than you do. When you have purpose, you get energy; you are not bored. Boredom brings depression and depression breeds contempt or saps your energy.

I don't like laziness. It's fine to lay around in a clean or straightened house. I think activities should be scheduled around work; not the opposite. I don't like selfish people. I don't think you are selfish, I think you don't think.

When you moved in, you knew our house was overflowing—full. You saw our closets were full. I gave you a closet that was almost empty. You asked me to move my few things that were in there (I heard what you were not saying), so you could hang up your dresses. I saw plenty of room in the closet, but I guess you didn't want your things to touch mine. Each one of our closets are packed like sardines. I moved my things and packed them into my already packed closet. I don't think you have noticed. If so, I didn't hear a thank you.

Enough of that! It's very unladylike to be arguing in public. Don't let anyone draw you into that. It's beneath you as a lady, a Christian, and an Alexander. Dignity is important. That's what makes a person beautiful; not their hair, color, looks or size.

We have a problem. Let me hear your side so we can find a solution.

Love, Grandma.

# CHAPTER TWENTY NINE

My friend called me today and as we talked it reminded my why we need some friends our own age.

She informed me that her husband had all his teeth pulled and was waiting on his full mouth of dentures. I could identify with that. Grandpa Alex lost two and a half, partial plates. One he lost somewhere in the house and has never found. The other, he sent to the cleaners and never saw them again either. The half one (his bottom ones) he left in a glass in a hotel room in Detroit.

Some of my younger acquaintances might think that this was funny, but they really wouldn't understand. They would probably wonder how he lost his teeth or that all old people lose their teeth and that it won't happen to them for another thirty-five years. You don't have to lose your teeth if you eat and brush properly and see your dentist twice a year.

So, have good hygiene, ride your bikes, swim, skate, run, or walk. Start now so it will be a habit when you are older. Many diseases can be controlled or prevented by eating correctly, having a positive attitude, and exercise. Negative feelings release poisons into your body, causing many ailments like ulcers, heart trouble, strokes, high blood pressure and many others.

Think about food. Most things that are wrong with you can be traced back to your eating habits: High cholesterol obesity, indigestion, heartburn, constipation, diarrhea. salmonella poisoning, food poisoning, etc.

When I was suffering with my joints, it was diagnosed as arthritis; but it was a vitamin deficiency. I needed calcium, but my body also needed Vitamin D so that it could process the calcium. I could have drank Vitamin

D fortified milk. Since my body doesn't like milk, I could have substituted it for Dairy Ease and not had joint problems.

I just wouldn't accept arthritis. Since I've been taking the vitamins and calcium, my joint pains have stopped, life has come back to both big toes and the charley horses are gone. I feel great! My obesity comes from too much food for the amount of exercise I get. My metabolism is sluggish so I should eat less and exercise more. I had an excuse because of my joints. Now that I have been healed, I have no reason other than habit or laziness now to be fat. I don't want to be too small, but I need and want to lose eighty pounds. I feel my best at a size eighteen. I went to a size fourteen once and I looked and felt sick.

Incident: 7/23/98. In church tonight Grandpa Alex embarrassed two young men, one sixteen and the other fourteen, who were talking to each other while he was teaching a lesson. He called them up and asked them to tell us what they were saying since it seemed to be more important than what he was saying. I thought that was a little harsh. One of the mothers left and I'm sure the parents and grandmother of the other child were embarrassed too. My heart sank. Maybe I'm too soft, but I suppose I would have handled it differently. God made mothers and fathers. Maybe I would have instructed the ushers to stop them from talking or asked one to move.

If the kids come back to church, and they probably will because their parents will, they might just be waiting until they are grown so they can give it up. The sixteen-year old isn't made to come to church so I hope he hasn't been turned off. He could be on the street, on drugs or in a gang but he chooses to come to church on a Thursday night for Bible study. I'm impressed when I see teenagers at church, for whatever the reasons. Maybe it's to see other young people, but they could see other young people at parks and on the street. So, I pray that these young people keep the faith and keep the desire to come to church and serve God.

One of those young men was one of your cousins. I pray for you all every day. And, if a prayer is a sincere desire of the heart, your salvation, health, mental and emotional well-being and your welfare is a constant prayer of mine. I love you so dearly and I pray for the best for you. Since I am abiding in Him and His word is abiding in me, I trust God that my prayers are answered. I don't believe that any of my kids . . . Mike and his family of five, Bart and his family of about twenty, Milton and his family of eight, Barry and his family of seven, Bretta and her family of three,

Byron and his family of seven, Judi and her family of five, Pat and her family of three, Charlene and her family of six, and Warren and his family of five . . . will be lost.

My case against abortion: One lady said she had a vision where unborn babies were corning up before the Lord and saying, "I would have been evangelist, doctor, great scientist, president, etc., but they wouldn't let me be born." If you have been a party to an abortion, ask God to forgive you and you forgive yourself. But don't make that your cure-all. One girl in my class said she has had eight (8) abortions. I didn't know you could have that many. She said pills gave her side affects.

There must be a reason and a purpose for your life. Seek until you find your reason for living. When you find your purpose, life will be meaningful and worth living. You can awake with enthusiasm and walk with a spring in your steps. Because you'll know there is a reason for your being.

# CHAPTER THIRTY

We had a group at Bloom Township High School in Chicago Heights. Nowadays you would call it a gang. The worst we did was eat pickles and cookies every morning and talk and giggle. We were all from the same religion. All the other girls were preparing for the prom or going to school games or having after-school activities. All of us were in the same boat—we couldn't date "unsaved" boys, couldn't wear makeup, and had to get permission to wear gym shorts and see the school movies. So we stuck together because we had a lot in common. Girls from a few other "White" religions had the same restrictions, so we all met during restricted gym.

We walked to and from school together. I lived closer to school so the girls picked me up last and dropped me off first. Going through the forest, which was the quickest way back and forth, the guys would taunt us. There was a "gang" of boys whose parents were "sanctified" also, but we called them backsliders. They smoked and said bad words (not in front of us) and acted roguish. They would position themselves between us and the other kids while we were walking home to protect us. They didn't say that's what they were doing, but we felt safe. Even though sometimes they would sing "Oh When The Saints Go Marching In". I felt proud. I don't know how the other girls felt. I liked being different.

Everyone in "the Heights" knew everyone. So we spoke to each other. People would sit on the porches, and coming home from the grocery store, you had to acknowledge everyone on the block. So when I moved to Chicago proper, I spoke to everyone. People looked at me like I was crazy. It's hard to break habits, so it took me a while to become a true Chicagoian. The last place I lived in Chicago I didn't even know any of my neighbors. I met a lady at a store and after hearing her address, I realized she lived upstairs over me and I had never seen her even though I had lived there over a year.

I moved to Minneapolis and found out that people wanted to speak. Nowadays people come to visit us and want to go to the Mall of America. In the seventies people came because they wanted to visit the Mayo Clinic. We were in a restaurant in the Kahler Hotel. A Black man (I know, we are "African Americans" now) passed the window and did a double take, came back and waved. We waved back. It occurred to me he was the only Black person we had seen in our over-night stay there. If this man lived in Rochester he might have been the only Black family there.

I used to take the kids to Rochester to learn the facts of life. They had educational movies at the museum across from the Mayo Clinic. We had fun. We went to the lake and saw thousands of birds, ducks and geese. We picnicked a lot. Sometimes we would leave church and go by Kentucky Fried Chicken and take it to the park. We did things together.

In those days I ate fast foods occasionally. Somewhere down the line, I started leaning towards being a vegetarian. I think it was when I first went on a "Daniel's fast" . . . no meat and no pleasant (sweet bread) bread. I took that as dessert. So for six weeks I didn't eat meat or sugar. I like being creative; so it was exciting seeing what I could cook that tasted good. I drank a little coffee with just cream, but tea became my drink. It tasted okay without sugar. I can't remember whether Equal was on the market in 1972.

Fruit satisfied my craving for sweets after a while. At first I had sugar withdrawals. That left in a week or so. Pasta, dairy, beans, salads and other vegetables sustained me. I tried tofu nut. I was unsuccessful. I could never get it to stay together. It looked like scrambled eggs in my food. I didn't eat fish or chicken. I saw that as meat. I was taking Amway Double X Vitamins and I felt good, physically, but I was glad when the six weeks were over.

# CHAPTER THIRTY ONE

## RECIPES

<u>Hot Water Cornbread</u>

2 Cups Corn Meal
1 Tbl. Sugar (or ½ teas. salt or 2 tsp. chicken bouillon or
any spice you like: onion salt, garlic powder etc.)
1 Cup Boiling Water

Mix dry ingredients, add hot water and mix well. Put
cooking oil in skillet (enough to cover the bottom), and
heat. Form each tablespoon of mixture with your hands
into an oblong ball and fry. Turn when brown. Should
make about 14. Serve with any vegetable or use as you
would cornbread.

<u>Cornbread Dressing/Stuffing</u>

4 Cups Corn Meal (I like yellow)
1 Cup Flour
4 Tsp. Baking Powder
6 Eggs (slightly beaten)
1/4 Cup Cooking Oil
1 Tsp. Salt
2 Cups milk (or enough so that bread is pourable)
Mix together. Pour into a greased pan. Cook in oven
at 375 for about 20 minutes or until brown. This bread

is not for eating; it will be too coarse. This is dressing cornbread.

### Actual Stuffing

Cornbread (the above)
3 Cups Diced Celery
2 Chopped Onions
2 Chopped Green Peppers
4 Chopped Garlic Cloves
4 Tsp. Sage
2 Quarts Chicken Bouillon
2 Sticks Margarine or Butter
4 Eggs Beaten

Mix all ingredients well, adding beaten eggs last, Pour into roasting pan (or stuff into a chicken or turkey), and cook at 325 (covered) for three hours. Make sure there is enough broth so the dressing won't be thy. Uncover for the last ½ hour. This is a good dressing for stuffed pork chops but eliminate all but ¼ stick of butter, Too much sage makes it bitter. The chicken and celery flavors make the dressing tasty, so increase or decrease to your liking. This is also good for turkey and chicken.

### Greens (Collard, Mustard, Turnip, Kale, Spinach and Swiss Chard)

6 Bunches
1 Greer Pepper (chopped)
1 Onion
3 Tbl. Lemon Pepper

I use Collards mostly because I am lazy. It takes less time to pick and wash them. I have mixed the greens. Once I mixed them all and added turnip bottoms.

Pick and wash the greens. Look for bugs and worms. Take off large stems and soak them in salt water (this will kill any bugs you might have missed). Wash greens four or five times; or until the water doesn't look cloudy or the sink doesn't feel sandy. Collard greens can be washed leaf by leaf. In a large pot, cook meat. You can use smoked ham hocks, salt pork, smoked turkey parts, or make it vegetarian by using lemon pepper, butter/margarine and pork seasoning (if you're not a purist). When the meat is half done, add the washed greens and other ingredients. Finish cooking the meat about 1-½ hours.

Greens make liquid so don't use too much water. Your taste and vitamins are in the juice. I add peeled and diced turnip bottoms to the greens at the beginning of cooking. I like strong, slightly bitter greens, but a tsp. of sugar will take away the bitterness. Spinach, Kale and Mustard are mild greens. Spinach and Kale should be added last since they only need to be cooked about 15 minutes. Experiment until you find the way you can eat them. Greens taste good with hot water cornbread, sliced tomatoes and onions. Boil some ears of corn and some candied yams and there's your meal.

## Frozen Greens

Boil ham hocks or meat. Cook the water down. Don't pour it out—this will take away the taste. Add bags of frozen greens, onions, green peppers, lemon pepper, salt and red pepper (optional). Cook until greens are done, about 1 hour. If you add diced turnip bottoms, it will give your greens more flavor.

## Candied Yams

3 Large Potatoes (peeled, washed and sliced)
1½ Cups Sugar
1 Tsp. Nutmeg
1 Stick Butter

I think I use sweet potatoes. Anyway, they are the light orange potatoes. I like the larger ones. Skinny ones are for baking.

In a pan sprayed with Pam, layer the potatoes and sugar, dart with butter, and sprinkle the nutmeg. Cover the pan and place in a preheated oven at 375 for ½ hour. Take off the cover and cook until the potatoes are bubbling with syrup. Cool and enjoy!

## Boiled Corn on the Cob

1 Bag Frozen Corn
2 Tsp. sugar

I like the frozen ears. Would you believe I used to shuck the corn? Even pick them from the stalks. I hate worms so frozen is good for me. Put on a pot of water. Add 2 tsp. of sugar. Put corn in boiling water. Boil for about five minutes.

## Pickled Okra

1 Box Frozen Okra
1 Tbl. Crushed Red Pepper
1 Cup Vinegar
½ Tsp. Salt
3 Clove Garlic
¼ Onion

In a saucepan bring all ingredients but Okra to a rolling boil. Put in Okra, cover and remove from heat. When cool, put in a container and refrigerate. Make sure mixture covers the Okra. Eat with greens, beans or any vegetable.

## Oven Fried Potatoes

    5, 6, or 7 Potatoes (peeled and cut up)
    1 Large Onion (diced)
    2 Tbl. Cooking Oil
    1 Tsp. Garlic Powder
    3 Tsp. Salt
    1 Tsp. Pepper

Mix salt, pepper, and garlic powder. Place potatoes and onion in a Pam-sprayed pan (potatoes should be rubbed in cooking oil). Sprinkle with seasoning and bake for ½ hour at 325 or until they start to brown. Stir once during cooking. They are good as breakfast potatoes or as the "starch" (what we called it in my day), at lunch or dinner.

## Skillet Fried Potatoes

    5, 6, or 7 Potatoes
    1 Large Onion (chopped)
    Salt (to taste)
    Pepper (to taste)
    ¼ Green Pepper
    2 Tbl. Cooking Oil

In a hot skillet add oil so that bottom is covered. (When skillet is tilted you should see about 2 Tbl. in the corner). I cook with a 12" skillet. Drop in all the above ingredients. Cover the pan and fry until potatoes are light brown. Turn the potatoes over and cook uncovered until the potatoes are brown. Stir them once or twice after they begin to brown. Serve and enjoy!

## Homemade Vegetable Soup

    3 Lbs. Stewing Beef
    6 Stalks of Celery (chopped)
    2 Green Peppers (chopped)
    3 Onions (chopped)
    5 Cloves Garlic
    2 Bay Leaves
    1 Tbl. Italian Seasoning
    1 Tbl. Parsley
    Salt to taste)
    Pepper (to taste)
    2 Qt. Water

Cook above ingredients until meat is done. In our home, the taste of celery, tomatoes and the beef flavoring makes the kind of soup that soothed the stomach, healed the sick, and curbed the hunger. Then during my "midlife crisis" I became an on-again, off-again vegetarian. Six weeks at a time I didn't eat meat at all. Now, I eat a little meat. If Alex orders a steak, I will order my vegetarian meal and take the tail off of his steak.

    Add:
    5 Potatoes (quartered)
    4 Carrots
    Cool for 10 additional minutes.
    Add:
    1 Large Can Crushed Tomatoes
    1 Large Can Tomato Sauce
    1 Large Frozen Mixed Vegetables
    Boil again for about five minutes.

    Add:
    1 Cup Curly Pasta
    Boil again.

Add:
1 Bag Frozen Broccoli or Cauliflower (or any other vegetable including cut Okra)

Cook for another five minutes and remove from heat. Serve with cornbread or crackers. Variations: You can use sauteed hamburger, chicken or no meat just beef bouillon. Try some of these vegetables for a different taste: 1 parsnip (peeled and cubed), 1 turnip bottom, ½ cabbage (cut). 1 cup rutabaga, whole, fresh tomatoes (that are too soil for eating), whole green beans, whole kernel corn, bok choy and mushrooms.

## Bread Pudding

> 1 Loaf Bread
> 1 Stick Butter (melted)
> 1 ¼ Cup Sugar
> ¼ Cup Honey
> 5 Eggs (beaten)
> 1½ Tsp. Cinnamon
> 1 Cup Raisins
> 1 Cup Chopped Walnuts

Preheat oven to 350. Spray a loaf pan with cooking spray (like Pam). 'Mix all ingredients, stir and beat for about one minute. Pour in loaf pan and cook for about 25 minutes or until golden brown. Cool for ten minutes before serving. Serve with whipped cream or any other topping.

If you cut the crust off of your sandwiches, save them in a baggie or bread bag so you'll know when you have a loaf. I am a convenience cook. I use what I have in the kitchen. Some of the children growing up in my house didn't like leftover's not realizing that seasonings have settled into the food and it usually tastes better the next day. So I freeze. Potatoes taste mealy after fleeting, so if you want to freeze soup, take out the potatoes. That's why I quarter the potatoes so I can find them easily. So here goes my cobbler recipe. I am also a quantity cook, so adjust the recipe to your specifications.

## Peach Cobbler

    4 Large Cans Sliced Peaches (juice also)
    2 ½ Cups Sugar
    1 1/2 Tsp. Nutmeg
    6 Cloves or ½ Tsp. Ground Cloves
    1 ½ Stick Butter
    1 Large Aluminum Pan
    2 Tsp. Flour

Pie Crusts (to cover bottom of pan, a few strips in peaches, and to cover the top)

In a large bowl mix all the ingredients. If you're going to use the pan again, spray it. Roll out the crust and position it around the bottom of the pan. Pour in the peach mixture. Put about six strips of crust in the mixture before you put the top on. This makes a thickening plus the strips will taste like dumplings when it's done. Cut the rest of the crust in strips and cover. Cover and connect the top and bottom and the edges of the pan. Cut them the size of the width of the pan. Cut the other lengthwise (you might have to use two to make one long enough). It doesn't have to be pretty because it will be when it's cooked and brown. Place this finished product in a preheated oven (400) for about 35 minutes or until brown. The juice should be thickened but not pasty when ready.

## Homemade Cake

    3 Cups Flour (sifted; I sift 4 times)
    1½ Sticks Butter
    3 Tsp. Baking Powder (2 level, 1 slightly more)

1 Tsp. Salt
4 Eggs (beaten)
1 ½ Cups Sugar
1 ½ Tsp. Vanilla flavoring (I like Watkins)
1¼ Cup Milk

Preheat oven to 350. Grease and flour three cake pans or one sheet cake pan. In a large bowl, cream butter and sugar with your hand (I use a disposable glove). The heat from your hands causes the butter and sugar to mix well. Cream it until it gleams. Stir in beaten eggs. In sifter, add flour and all the dry ingredients. Alternate dry ingredients with milk. Mix well, then beat until well mixed and smooth. (I used to do this with a mixing spoon before I had an electric mixer). Pour batter into the pans and bake about ½ hour or until you can stick a toothpick into the center of the cake and it comes out clean. Let cool about 15 minutes before putting the frosting on. I used to make my own. And since I don't really like a lot of gook. I buy the frosting then serape most of it off of my piece of cake. It would be nice to try this scratch cake at least once, then graduate to one of the boxed cakes; the pudding in the mix kind but use milk instead of water and add a little flavoring (maybe a little butter). Enjoy your day without all the trouble—tastes just as good!

## Rice Pudding

3 Cups Rice
1 Cup Sugar
¾ Stick Butter
1 Tsp. Vanilla Flavoring
½ Tsp. Nutmeg
1 Cup Raisins (optional)
3 Eggs (slightly beaten)

Mix all ingredients. Put into a greased pan. Bake at 350 for ½ hour.

## Left Over Rice

What to do with leftover rice: put it in a stir fly, add to soup, meat loaf, serve it as a cereal for breakfast with sugar, butter and milk, or eat it for breakfast instead of potatoes with butter and salt or make a gravy of onions, green peppers, salt, water, flour and brown gravy master. Pour over rice, yum!!

## No-Cook Banana Pudding

2 Bunches Ripe Bananas (about 10 in all)
3 Boxes Vanilla Wafers
2 Large Boxes Vanilla Instant Pudding
3 Small Boxes Banana Instant Pudding
2 Small Boxes Coconut Instant Pudding
10 Cups Milk
1 Tsp. Vanilla Flavoring

Follow the box directions for pudding mix. I used to make my own custard until I discovered Jell-O Instant Pudding. Layer the bottom of an aluminum pan with wafers. Place sliced bananas next, then pudding mix. Repeat process. End with pudding mix. Refrigerate for two hours before serving.

## Sweet Potato Pie

4 Large Sweet Potatoes (boiled)
1 Cup Sugar
2 Cans Eagle Brand Condensed Milk
2 Sticks Butter
8 Eggs (separated. yolk beaten slightly, white beaten till fluffy)

1 Tsp. Nutmeg (don't use cinnamon, it makes the
   pies dark)
1 Can Carnation Milk
8 Frozen Pie Crust Pans (I use Deep Dish Pet Ritz)

Cut peeled sweet potatoes crosswise. Add sugar, butter and Eagle Brand milk. Beat until all the strings from the potatoes have been caught in the mixer. You will have to clean the mixer several times during the mixing. Taste to see if it's sweet enough. It should taste sweeter than you really like it because it loses some of its sweetness during cooking. Taste before you add the raw eggs because raw eggs can be dangerous. Next add the egg yolks and other ingredients, beat until smooth. Fold the fluffy egg whites into the mixture. Pour in pie pans. Put into preheated oven (400) and bake for 55 minutes or until a toothpick comes out clean.

## Green Beans

2 Packs Frozen Whole Green Beans
3 Tbl. Pork Flavoring Seasoning
1 Tbl. Butter
1 Onion
3 Tbl. Lemon Pepper
4 Peeled Potatoes (quartered)

Cook green beans for 15 minutes in one quart of water. Add all the ingredients and cook for about ½ hour. You may want to add some salt and pepper.

## Dry Beans

1 Lb. Mixed Beans
1 Gallon Water
1 Onion
Celery
Ham Hocks
Garlic

Carrots
1 Green Pepper

Pick, sort and wash beans. Soak overnight. Put washed beans in water with washed ham hocks. Add all other ingredients. Boil for five minutes. Turn down to low and cook for about three hours. Stir occasionally. For the last ½ hour, turn the heat up and let the beans and liquid thicken. Serve with Hot Water Cornbread.

## Cabbage

1 head Cabbage
Butter
1 Onion
1 Green Pepper
Lemon Pepper
Salt
Cut and wash cabbage. Add all ingredients to a greased skillet. Stir-fry.

## Smothered Chicken

1 Whole Chicken
2 Tbl. Butter
4 Tbl. Flour
Salt (to taste)
Pepper (to taste)
2 Cups Water

Pick out feathers and hairs. Soak overnight in the refrigerator in a little salt and water. Wash chicken. Season with salt (just a little since you soaked already). Coat it with flour (use more flour if you have to). Place in a greased pan. Add two cups water and cover. Bake at 325 for 1 ½ hours. Look at the chicken in 45 minutes to see if it needs the additional 45 minutes. Chicken should be well done. Do not reuse the utensils you used for the chicken without thoroughly washing them.

## Fried Chicken

> 1 Whole Chicken
> 2 Tbl. Butter
> 4 Tbl. flour
> Salt (to taste)
> Pepper (to taste)
> 4 Cups Cooking Oil
> Seasoning Salt (to taste)
> Garlic Powder (to taste)

Do the same as the Smothered Chicken but use a fry pan that is half full of cooking oil (about four cups). When it is hot enough, drop in the coated chicken. Brown chicken. Turn and brown the other side. Make sure the chicken is not red. I use the oven sometimes to keep the chicken hot while continuing to cook (if need be).

## Baked Chicken

> 1 Whole Chicken
> Seasoning Salt (to taste)
> Pepper (to taste)

Wash and soak chicken (see Smothered Chicken instructions). Season chicken with Seasoning Salt inside and out. Bake covered at 350 for one hour. Take cover off for the last 15 to 20 minutes for browning.

## Beef Roast

> 1 Beef Roast
> Tenderizer Seasoning
> Celery
> 1 Onion

1 Green Pepper
Garlic
Potatoes
Carrots
Salt (to taste)
Pepper (to taste)
½ Cup Flour
3 Cups Cold Water

Wash and soak meat. Use a little tenderizer. Follow the directions. Cut up celery, onion, green pepper, garlic, potatoes and carrots. Season with salt and pepper. Flour the roast. Put all ingredients in roasting pan. Add flour to water. Pour over all ingredients. Add brown gravy mix. Cover and cook for two hours in oven (350).

## Steak

1 Round Steak
Tenderizer
Salt (to taste)
Pepper (to taste)
½ Cup Flour
½ Cup Cooking Oil
1 Onion (diced)
1 Cup Water

Wash and soak meat. You can make the steak tender enough to fry by using the side of a plate and beating it, if you don't have tenderizer. Cut into individual sizes and season with salt and pepper. Coat with flour. Fry and brown on both sides. When all the steak is browned return it to the skillet. Add onion and water. Simmer on low. Serve.

## Pork Chops

1 Pack Pork Chops

Lemon Pepper (to taste)
Seasoning Salt (to taste)
½ Cup Flour

Wash and soak meat. Season chops with lemon pepper and a little seasoning salt. Coat with flour. You can fry, bake or broil.

Peas

1 Bag Frozen Green Peas
1 Tbl. Sugar
3 Tbl. Butter
Follow directions on bag. Add sugar and butter.

## Corn

1 Bag/Can Corn
1 Tbl. Sugar
3 Tbl. Butter
2 Tbl. Flour

Boil the corn with a small amount of water. Stir in flour and butter, which has been mixed in a skillet. Add corn to the butter mixture. Cook until the liquid in the corn is smooth.

## Veggie Burgers

3 Lbs. Hamburger
1 Onion (chopped)
1 Green Pepper (chopped)
Pepper (to taste)
3 Cans Vegetarian Vegetable Soup

Saute hamburger, onion and green pepper. Drain off any excess liquid and grease. Add three cans condensed soup and pepper. Do not add water, Cook for about ten minutes to let the flavors blend. Serve over mashed potatoes or rice.

## Meat Loaf

3 Lbs. Hamburger
15 Saltine Crackers or ¾ Cup Oatmeal
4 Eggs (beaten slightly)
½ Cup Celery (chopped)
1 Large Onion (chopped)
1 Green Pepper (chopped)
½ Tsp. Garlic Powder
1½ Tsp. Black Pepper
½ Cup Milk (I use evaporated)
2 Cups Ketchup
2 Cups Cheese (chopped)
4-5 Stalks Frozen Broccoli
2 Tsp. Salt

In large mixing bowl put all the ingredients but cheese, broccoli and one cup ketchup. Mix well. Spray a loaf pan with Pam. Put in half of the mixture. In the middle, put the broccoli and cheese. Put in the rest of the mixture making sure the top and bottom layers are sealed (mashed together). Spread the last cup of ketchup over the mixture. Cover and place in the oven at 350 for one hour. The last 15 minutes uncover so meatloaf can brown. Let cool. Slice and serve with spaghetti or mashed potatoes. It looks pretty too with the broccoli and cheese!

## Spaghetti Sauce

3 Onions (chopped)
5 Cloves Garlic (chopped)
2 Green Peppers (chopped)
4 Tbl. Bouillon
2 Large Cans Tomato Sauce

1 Tbl. Oregano
3 Tbl. Parsley Flakes
1 Tbl. Italian Seasoning
Salt and Pepper (to taste, but beware because of
    bouillon)
3 Tbl. Cooking Oil
½ Tsp. Onion Powder
½ Tsp. Garlic Powder

Sauté first three ingredients in cooking oil. Add seasoning. Transfer to a larger pot. Add tomato sauce and simmer for two hours (if you have the time). Serve over pasta. To save on the sauce, sometimes I mix it in the spaghetti. Experiment with different size spaghetti noodles with other noodles.

Instant Mashed Potatoes

1 Box Instant Mashed Potatoes
Milk
Butter
Salt (to taste)
Pepper (to taste)

Follow the boxed directions. Use milk instead of water. Add extra butter. Salt and pepper to your liking.

Eggs Scrambled With Cheese

1-6 Eggs (beaten)
Cheese (to taste; I use Sharp cheese-one chunk to
    ¼ cup shredded)
2 Strips Green Pepper (red or yellow)
Butter (enough to coat skillet)
1 Tbl. Milk
Salt (to taste)
Pepper (to taste)

Mix all ingredients. Stir in skillet until cheese is melted. Serve.

Party Punch (A Favorite!)

- 1 Bottle Ginger Ale
- 1 Can pineapple Juice
- 1 Can Chunk Pineapple
- 1 Jar Maraschino Cherries (red, green or both)
- 4 Cups Water
- 6 Cinnamon Sticks
- 2 Tbl. Rum Flavoring

Freeze one ice tray of ginger ale and one tray of pineapple juice. Freeze chunk pineapple and the maraschino cherries. In a punch bowl put frozen ingredients. Pour in the rest of the ginger ale and the can of pineapple juice. In a saucepan boil the water. Add the cinnamon sticks. Simmer for ten minutes. Let cool then add rum flavoring. Just before serving add one cup cinnamon sticks to punch bowl. Very festive and tasty!

Potato Salad

- 5 Lbs. Potatoes
- 6 Eggs
- ½ Cup Onion (finely diced)
- ½ Cup Pepper (finely diced and mix the colors)
- ¼ Cup Sweet Pickles (finely diced)
- 2 Tbl. Pimento (diced)
- ½ Cup Sandwich Spread
- ½ Cup French Dressing
- ¼ Cup Mustard
- 1 Tbl. Sugar
- ¼ Tsp. Salt
- Pepper (optional, to taste)
- 1 Tbl. Paprika (optional)

Boil potatoes in jacket. Cool then peel and dice. Boil eggs, cool then chop. Mix all ingredients. I use disposable gloves so I can mix with my hands. Use more sandwich spread if needed. I use paprika for coloring. Chill and serve.

## Oven Baked Ribs

1 Slab Ribs
1 Jar Barbecue Sauce
1 Large Onion (sliced)
1 Large Green Pepper (sliced)
Garlic Powder (to taste)
Seasoning Salt (to taste)
Red Pepper (to taste)

Wash and season ribs with last three seasonings. Season enough to cover both sides. Put in refrigerator overnight. Transfer to a roasting pan and cook at 375 in the oven for 45 minutes. Take out and drain off grease. Add barbecue sauce of your choice. Cook for another 45 minutes or until tender.

## Stuffed Green Peppers

1 Lb. Lean Ground Beef
¼ Lb. Ground Turkey
¼ Lb. Pork Sausage
½ Onion (chopped)
½ Green Pepper (chopped)
2 Stalks Celery (chopped)
¼ Tsp. Salt
Pepper (to taste)
½ Cup Ketchup
¼ Cup Rice (uncooked)
½ Cup Whole Kernel Corn
5 Green Peppers

Spray bread pan with Pam. Preheat oven to 375. Cut green peppers lengthwise. Mix all ingredients. Fill peppers. It's okay to pile them high. Cover with foil and cook for ½ hour. Uncover and cook another 15 minutes or until brown and done. Let peppers cool for about 10 minutes before serving.

## Stuffed Baked Potatoes

5 Large White Potatoes (boiled not mashed)
¼ Cup Evaporated Milk
½ Stick Butter
¼ Cup Sharp Cheese
Salt (to taste)
Pepper (to taste)
1 Cup Cheese (shredded)

Boil potatoes, then cool. Cut potato lengthwise. Scrape out as much of the potato as you can leave the potato half in tact. In a bowl mix all ingredients. Beat and mash until smooth. Season the potato shells then fill with the mixture Bake on a cookie sheet at 325 for ½ hour. Sprinkle with remaining cheese and bake for another 15 minutes or until cheese is melted.

## Salmon Croquettes

1 Can Pink Salmon
1 Onion (chopped)
2 Garlic Cloves (chopped)
¼ Green Pepper (chopped)
2 Eggs (beaten)
½ Tsp. Salt
½ Tsp. Black Pepper
¼ Tsp. Cayenne Pepper (optional)
¾ Cup Cornmeal (not Jiffy)
1 Cup Cooking Oil

Mix all ingredients. Put enough oil in skillet to cover bottom. Make patties from salmon mixture. Place in hot skillet. When salmon is brown on one side, turn over and evenly brown on other side. After pan is heated turn burner to medium temperature so onions will be tender.

I was talking to someone yesterday and we were not connecting. I just asked her an opinion on a subject. She started analyzing and then saying she couldn't second guess someone else's actions. I missed my friend who had died nine months before. Even though I had been talking to this person for forty years, we could only communicate on things that were of interest to her.

My dead friend and I could talk on many levels. Even on levels which we differed on. We never made each other feel dumb or feel that your subject was not one to be talked about. It wasn't always like this. We developed this relationship. I decided that day that I would find me a talking buddy. I need to talk and to unburden myself. I would like someone to respond to me, but I grew up an only child so I remember telling my thoughts to pen pals all over the world. My secrets I wrote, read, cried and tore them up.

So I needed an avenue to vent and get my ideas out of me and into the universe. I have a tree outside of my bedroom window. The tree covers the bulk of my patio window. I have been watching the birds for months. I watch their habits. They wake me up in the morning and I see if they are home nearing dusk. There are storm warnings today and they are not home in the tree. I wonder where they go during crisis. But the tree is there waving in the wind and seemingly secure unless we experience stronger winds.

Since I have been looking at this tree for almost twenty years, I feel it is a part of my life. I have never talked to it, but what harm could it do. It might take some time getting used to it, but it took time getting used to my friend.

I have family and friends, but no one person knows me, and I don't know anyone I would trust with all of the valuables of my thoughts. Vince, my dead friend, went through the changes with me. He knew many of my thoughts. I never opened myself up all the way to anyone. I think there are some things you only tell God.

So my tree will hear my thoughts and concerns. (Can a tree hear?) Since I will be talking to it daily until I have made up for lost time, let's name it. I want to be able to say "good morning and goodnight" to a name. I don't know whether it is an oak or elm tree and I don't care. So I will give it a name that is dear to me. I like men, maybe because I was raised by my father—a good father. I always wanted a brother, so I adopted some. Vince was one of those brothers. I want a name that has a special meaning for me. I had a brother-in-law and a step-brother both named James. I said I was raised an only child, but I had many siblings by my father. I loved both of these James' very much. James Daughrity was murdered and James Morris disappeared. Then there was my grandfather whose name was Simon Perkins, a dear Sea Islander who outlived three wives and was a great father and grandfather. He and my grandmother taught me how to have a good marriage. I think I will call my tree Simon.

Hello, Simon, my name is Ruby. I need you desperately and I know you will listen when I bounce things off of you. I know the answer is within me, but I need to express and release these feelings. I know you won't mind how long I talk. It won't matter that I break a few verbs or change subjects in midstream. Since I am older I have to say things as they come to my mind or I might lose them. It's not the "old folks" disease. It's because I have put so much in my memory bank—and it can only hold fifty things. When fifty one gets on, number one drops off, so I am not claiming anything negative. I know that you, Simon, won't judge me no matter what I say or how I say it. I might think one way today and another way tomorrow, but you won't care. That's the way Vince was. He knew that people had a right to change their minds. He also knew that I was consistent about my values and my belief in God. I never wavered. You wouldn't even care if I questioned Him.

When I met Vince he was in college but a heroin addict. He was just getting out of prison. He was on a program called New Careers. I was working for Twin Cities Opportunity Industrialization Center (TCOIC). His team was interning at our center. One day he passed out in front of the building and was taken to the hospital. I was from a small town and was taught to visit the sick. I went to the hospital to visit Vince. He was so impressed that I would take the time to see about him. He couldn't understand that a person who didn't know him and didn't want anything from him could be for real. Surely I must want something. He was a player, so maybe I wanted him. When he came back to work he lifted every leaf to find my motives. He took me home sometimes after work. He ate lunch with me at work. Vince picked my brain. He finally figured out that I was the kind of Christian who believed that everyone I came in contact with was a "soul." I knew that he had too much going for him to remain on the road he was traveling. Some nights when he was high he would stop by our house. Husband would play the piano. I would put on the coffee pot and the kids would sing for him. When he was satisfied, he would leave and that would be about four in the morning. Gradually he would put down his habits and finish school. He became a licensed social worker and drug counselor.

So Simon, my life is complicated and full so I will be spending a lot of time with you.

Should I start from the time I couldn't talk to Vince anymore? I could never talk to anyone about how I felt when he died. Just the thought of that statement made me tired. Maybe I won't start there. Maybe somewhere that I didn't go with Vince.

My undisciplined inconsistent life frustrates me, but not enough to change. Husband said if a dog is lying on a nail and is howling, he will get off the nail when it hurts him enough. So I am not frustrated enough to discipline myself. The discipline I need is my weight. I need to be consistent with my eating and exercise habits.

Well, my birds are home. So goodnight Simon.

Good morning, Simon. I didn't hear the birds this morning. I must have slept in. I thought I would listen to the messages on the phone and to my surprise and delight I heard a message from one of my precious spirited sons. I haven't heard from him since the choir went to Houston on April 5, 2006. He's a recovering crack addict. He was doing so well. He brought his family in. His number was changed and I couldn't get in touch with him. He was such an asset to the church. Very vocal, talented, and caring. He has had several relapses, but this was the longest. My heart ached for him like many mothers' would. I returned his call. He was so happy to hear from me as I was to be talking to him. We were both crying. I told him that I loved him, missed, him, needed him and wanted him. I also asked him to sit by me on Sunday (hoping he was coming) so I can protect him from non-thinking, self-righteous, compassionless, well meaning people. I promised to beat them up if they swarmed him.

I don't have a narcotic addiction but one Lenten season I gave up sugar and did I pay. I had withdrawals. I had no energy. I could hardly lift my arms. I was sleepy and lethargic, and because I don't drink coffee without sugar, I had a double trouble. Caffeine and sugar. I know this is nothing compared to crack, but my imagination can magnify this 10,000 times. I can have compassion. I knew that in forty days I could resume life as usual, if I wanted to. I could also choose to stay free, since the chemicals are out of my body.

Simon, I don't understand the drug culture, but I know the ones who are victims and caught in the web are human beings, God's creations, and with tender loving care can find a way to recovery. I know that many will fall through the cracks, but let me keep the ones entrusted in my care. I have prayed that the ones who pass through our paths will make it. Presumptuous? No, we might not be the ones to finish the job or to even see the finished product, but we ask that someone somewhere be placed in their paths that will be the positive influence they need.

Just like it takes a village to raise a child, it takes all of the family of God to go to the aid of hearts that were wounded in the cradle. Meet people where they are and love them through to health.

Health, what is it? Is anyone totally healthy? Just as clean is relative. I know there is a standard and the bible is a Christian's standard. I heard a relative pray a prayer of thankfulness. He thanked God for a reasonable portion of health. My aunt used to reply after being asked how she was feeling—"tolerable." To her that was health. A reasonable portion of health could mean "that's all I expect." Or all I deserve. Sometimes, Simon, I think people are like that in everyday living. I have money for my necessities, so why be greedy and ask or expect more? I believe that God has put enough creativity in each of us to live more than hand to mouth. Choices have made us passive and content with what we have or don't have.

I see so much waste, maybe because these last two generations haven't seen the worst times. I've been through several wars—WW II, Korean and Vietnam. I remember the stamps for meat, sugar, gas, etc. I remember rinsing out the tomato paste cans to get the last drop. You saved bread crust for bread pudding, the corn bread for dressing. The vegetables were saved for soup or stew. You made your own liquid soap with too small bar soap placed in a jar of water. So with the waste, we have to go to the stores more often leaving less to save or use for other needed things.

I have seen some people clean and just do the surface. No dusting, no mopping, just sweep and put the rug down. That is their version of clean. I have also seen people use religion like that. Their own brand, setting their own standards. And I don't have a right to judge or condemn anyone. Wherever they are on their journey as long as they are moving towards a positive finish line.

Oh, enough philosophing. I was talking about my spiritual son. Just hearing his voice today gave me joy.

I've got to go to the prison volunteer training tonight. We have to retrain every year. We have been going to this prison for more than ten years. My prison work began when I was 15 years old in Illinois. I went to Joliet, Pontiac, Stateville and county jail until I moved to Minnesota in 1967. We started going to Stillwater, Sandstone, and Duluth. We went to Red Wing, St. Cloud, and the federal prison in Rochester. Lino was on our list also. We also go to St. Joe's Home for Children and to the St. Croix Boot Camp in New Richmond, Wisconsin. So I gladly go to this training tonight, because prison work is very dear to me. We help them after the fact, but on the outside we are very much into prevention.

None of my stress stems from ministering to the ones that have been put into my life. It comes from paying bills to keep a place open for them to gather. A house of refuge. A sanctuary. No matter how many people that are being helped, they have limited amounts of money to help with mortgage, lights, gas, phone, supplies and so on.

Simon, I can't tell everyone this and especially husband that I have taken our retirement money to take care of the place where the prevention takes place. Sixty percent of the people who frequent this place are thirty and under. For the last two months this has happened. I've done what some people do with their spiritual lives. Clean up the outside and leave the inside raving. I have kept the physical side opened, lights are on and phone, etc., but insurance, lawyers, printing, taxes and the meatier things are lacking.

Oh, I am stressed. People think the church is raking in the money. They don't know how many empty envelopes are in the basket. People are ashamed not to be giving so they take the envelope and take it to the front. I have cried many times counting the offering when I found two cents, or food stamps, when they were giving them out. I have found bus tokens, first class stamps, coupons, etc. I have cried that they have given what they had and I prayed for them and wished God would honor their efforts. It made me love the ministry more and I would lay down my all to see them "safe."

They know that I would never tell anyone who gave what and that I would never look down on them, but be proud of them for sharing what they had. I can't tell you how much I love them. They know from the smiles, hugs, and shoulders to cry on I offer.

My job at the prison is to sit at the door and be the bathroom monitor. They have to go one at a time. Since touching is forbidden for the residents, I sit there and give them a hug as they wait for their turn to go potty. I think some of them wait in line for the hug.

The rest of the team is singing and preaching or some other part of the ministry, but I have chosen this position. I have done everything in the church from cleaning toilets to preaching, and nothing satisfies me more than teaching the young adults in Sunday school and being the bathroom monitor.

I don't know what's going to happen about the bills. I do know that this too shall pass away! What is faith? I think it takes a lot of energy to have faith—especially for yourself. It is easier to have faith for others. I have seen miracles happen when I agree with others about their conditions. We pray and forget about it. I expect a positive report and most of the time I get it. I don't have to hear the bill collectors, or feel the turbulence, or see the wounds.

So I pray for a miracle and actually look for and expect one, and the bills kept coming. Since I am responsible and believe that I should obey the laws of the land—should I park the cars after the thirty-day grace period? Should I let the phones be turned off and let everyone know we're in trouble, or should I shoulder this alone? We have a board and ninety percent of them pay their tithes. That's all the Lord requires—tithes and offerings. When I tell the group that the bills are behind, they know they are doing their share and since we have a policy of not begging I have always thought that it cheapens God by having chicken dinners, etc. I believe in praying and trusting. I have since moved that stone and given the people free reign. I have written proposals and letters with little response.

So, Simon, what is faith? I have hoped for things not seen. I have asked, knocked and went seeking. I am not discouraged and won't give up. I am just looking for the right formula. I know there is a key. We have a good product. I just don't know how to market it. I am good at what I am good at, but I need help in this department. When people get to where they can help us financially and with the business part, they leave and go to a more progressive church. I am happy to have been a part in their growth. We were organized to be the liaison between the street and the church. The dressing up place. A place to learn a few rules like not walking in and out of church when the speaker is up. Sometimes even to keep quiet during the sermon. How not to shimmy like "Sister Kate" when they get emotional, etc.

Simon, it is 4:20 a.m. on a Friday morning. I know the birds are fast asleep, but it is nearing their wake up time. I fell asleep in my big chair about 1 a.m. I went to the prison training Thursday night. We have to go every year. There were about twenty-five volunteers, three of which were new. I learned it was okay to let two women go to the toilet together, if I was on the inside with them. That even things we think are harmless could be considered contraband so a nothing in—nothing out is the policy. If a poem is read and a resident asks you for a copy, don't give it to them unless you have enough for everyone in attendance. Show no favoritism. Even giving someone a bible could be a violation. Instead donate it to the library so all may use it. Love them without getting personal. Even a mint should not be taken in. I eat a lot of garlic. I betcha I won't get as many hugs. Listerine just lasts so long. In my childhood there were nasty little black seed-like things. I might have to look those up. We rode to the training with one of our teammates. He got us home in record time. Remember Sunday when I was totally broke, well, today I could have stopped for coffee, but we got home in record time, he has a young wife!

A son took our bible class tonight and he came over to report how it went. Our company left about midnight and I was too comfortable to go to bed. As my habit is, I came in from the prison training and took of my street clothes and got ready for bed. I am lying across the bed now, very cold. The air is on low. So I must say goodnight—even if it is morning—it is yet dark. I need to get under the cover—and I will add an extra comforter. It is July 20th and we just recovered from a heat spell. The fires are yet burning in the Boundary Waters. I couldn't comprehend the acreage that was burnt, but it was put in perspective when they reported how many miles had been affected (30). That's as far as my house is from the Wisconsin border. There were no lives lost, but what about the animals? Where did they go and how many of their lives were lost?

I am a frustrated vegetarian.

Good morning, Simon. I don't see my birds. They probably left during the disturbing phone call I had this morning. In fact I really need to talk to Vince I need some feedback. In fact as I was waiting for the coffee I looked at my e-mail. Boy did I get a doozy. Coffee can wait. I have to talk while it is fresh.

Both are equally serious and Ruby #1 is raging so the first thing you'll hear will be from her. She needs to be validated and then curtailed. Is that a contradiction?

First I caught a spiritual son and daughter who hold offices in a church in a compromising situation. They are both separated from their spouses. I had been told by the man that there was one discretion. I didn't share this information. I heard remorse, we prayed and business as usual. I am not the one to be suspicious. I heard about chance meetings because the man told other people he hated himself for doing it, but not enough to quit. (Ruby #1) What was so disgusting was they grew up like brother and sister. We were at a party and I missed them both. I went to the apartment and they were there. I told them that I wasn't judging them—other than their common sense and their sense of timing. That was judging, wasn't it? Both of them deal with the sacraments of their church. I wouldn't have been involved if the man had not chosen to involve me. Did he need counseling or did he think it therapeutic to talk? Was he bragging? I'm an older woman, why did he feel like baring his soul to me? He had peers who he could have confessed to. I don't know if I saw remorse or "I got caught." The lady hasn't shown any regrets! I think she is proud of the little piece she got. What am I to say or advise? Am I to suggest they stop handling the sacraments until they get themselves together? I believe that most men think with the head of their penis and that the dumbest woman is smarter than the smartest man. #1 and #2 believe this.

Observation: Adam gave up his empire for Eve. King David couldn't stand to see a woman take a bath. He came down from his high road and took a gutter road and had sex with her and had her husband killed. Samson, the strongest man, couldn't lay his head in a woman's lap without revealing all of his secrets. Solomon, the one who was so wise, let 1,000 women lure him away from his purpose. The King of England stepped down from his throne for Wallis Simpson. A preacher lost his ministry for one piece and another one lost his following just for a look.

I can't remember a woman making such a sacrifice for the love of a man. Oh, they might leave a husband or even children, but I wonder how many have left their empire for the love of a man.

So what am I to do with this couple? Should I suggest they sit themselves down at their church until they can get it together or should I just pray and stay out of it? Is it my business? What about the young people that they are role models to?

I suggested to the man to take a couple of weeks off and romance his family. His bachelor pad just isn't working. He could win his wife back if he wanted to and it is worth the try. He called me back and tried to lay a guilt trip on me. "I know I have committed the unpardonable sin. I feel lower than low. I deserve this!" I assured him that it was indeed against our values and against the bible, but I wasn't a judge. Because he went over the boundaries there should be some consequences. Since I was the one who knew it, I thought it was best for him to remove himself for a few days on his own so he can reflect on his behavior. When he makes a decision, he can inform the leaders. I didn't think it would be wise for him to have a wife and a sleeping partner.

One thing that bothered me was his confession to another man at the church who had staggered the rules several years ago. This man called me and his lack of compassion was profound. One day maybe I can tell you about that because I gave him an assignment. Think of a consequence for this situation and let's compare notes. I told him that Nathan in the bible brought a problem to King David. David handed down a harsh sentence until Nathan told him he was the offender. Then he begged for mercy. It will be interesting to see what he comes up with.

Then my friend e-mailed me. She's been married about three months and her adjustment is not easy. After much dialogue I reminded her that a new pair of shoes is not as comfortable as a pair you have had for years. In fact they are probably your favorite pair. Marriage with time can become like your foot has been poured into a well-supported foam mattress. Even the romance can stand the test. Marriage is work and most of the time worth it. Isn't it exciting to find another person born into another family with different morals, values, habits, joys, sorrow, wisdom, understanding, knowledge and things that makes sense to them. You love red meat and he's a vegetarian. You like a house squeaky clean and he's junky. You are a book lover and he's never read a book. He likes spicy food and you want it bland. You can't cook and he's an excellent cook. He wants you to wash and iron his clothes and you can't see yourself doing this task. Isn't it intriguing putting this puzzle together? You like drama and he likes horror. What an adventure finding a safe meadow to graze in. Sometimes a little left of the track and sometimes a little right until you both find the middle of the road. Never really meshing—then you'd be bored with each other.

Oh, Simon, I forgot I was talking to you. I got carried away talking to my friend. I went grocery shopping today. It is not one of my favorite things since Vince died. Bretta took me. She was on the phone. We went to breakfast at Milda's. No complaints. It is not the place to go if you want to hold a conversation with the person you are with. It is a family owned, neighborhood restaurant. They lost their lease several years ago and had no choice but to close, but there was such an outcry from the community that investors heard and we now have a better place than before. I usually get a pasty but this was a breakfast day—grits and all. We left there and went to the Farmer's Market. There were so many people there that we kept on driving. I sometimes get my meat at Byerly's and my vegetables at Cub. Bretta was back on the phone and in my mind I had decided that I would get everything at Byerly's. I didn't feel like packing my own groceries and all the work of taking it out to my car. I am 70 years old and I think I deserve the courtesy of Byerly's. Byerly's and Lunds are going organic. I first recognized that when I was buying collard greens. At least 70 cents more a bunch organic.

One day I walked into the store and saw a beautiful display of green tomatoes. I got about six large ones. I was shocked when I got to the register and they were $23.00. Had I not been ashamed I would have changed my mind about Fried Green Tomatoes. Since I bought them, I used every one. Even the last one which had started to ripen. I seasoned them like fish and coated them with corn meal. I fried them until golden brown—turning them once. I served them with breakfast meat and toast. Delicious if you like that sort of food.

I gave Bretta the dairy and grocery list. I went to the meat, produce and frozen food departments. We finished in half the time. Part of Vince's and my therapy was shopping—the Dollar Store, groceries, GNC and different outlet stores. Now I just want to get the shopping over with.

Simon, I am going through a dry spell spiritually. My bible reading is down and my patience with "fill in the spaces" is gone. Could it be that I am seventy and have been seeing and hearing the same "stuff" for sixty years? I want to be candid, but not stupid and irreverent? First let me say that I do have a good relationship with the Lord. I have given my heart to Jesus and He is my role model and God is my higher power. I talk (pray) to God in the name of Jesus often throughout the day. Most of them are not formal prayers. I talk to Him as I would a very special friend—more so because His spirit is living inside of me. I read in Romans that God has put a little of Him in each of us. He said if a person has never heard of Him and lives according to the dictates of his conscious, he would be saved. Romans 2:12-16. So I pray in my thoughts, desires, mannerisms and with my mouth. I learned the Acts ways—adoration, confession, thanksgiving and supplication. Also the finger way—one for God, nation, fellow man, etc. I've learned the screaming way—sometimes in distress you might have to just holler. Help! I would hate for my friend to have a formula to talk with me. Some conversations are just confessions. Sometimes it's just loving God. Thinking of where I might have been had we not embraced each other thinking of the pit I was in with an alcoholic father and a mother who had abandoned me. How I was raped at twelve. Why did He choose me? I am thankful and I love Him. So my prayers are spontaneous and personal. It is different than my talking to you, Simon. You can't do anything—not even listen (I don't think) but God is a person surrounding me and at the same time sitting on the throne of my heart (most of the time) the times that He isn't is my choosing—not His. Sorry, Simon, I got off on a tangent. I was talking about my dry spell. Several years ago during Lent I gave up things, but I also took on two special things. For forty days I drank two cups of coffee in the morning and couldn't/wouldn't drink anything else until I drank eight glasses of water. The other thing was to read one book of the bible each day during those forty days. Diligently I read the books. I found the shortest ones and when they were all gone I started on the longer books. By the 36th day I was inundated with the bible. I was fed up to my eyeballs. Have you ever eaten until one more bite would gag you? Well, shamefully saying this, I couldn't read another word. It had nothing to do with God. I wasn't sick of Him—just of the bible. Me who used to use the bible as a magic touch. Sleeping with it under my pillow, opening it and getting a saying for the day. Repeating promises for my life. Keeping a testament in my purse, in my desk and hiding the words in my heart. The bible tells us to be temperate in all things. I overdid it.

Then counting hearing sermons, I have coined myself as "the most preached to person in the world!" The average of going to church three times a week not counting revivals, conferences, radio, TV tapes, videos, and my husband is a preacher—so home. Let's say 10,000. From intellectual, hip hop, to emotional hackers. I have liked the variety. Just like music Alex used to sing in two quartets—The Holy Travelers and The Golden Swans. The Travelers were the opening group many times for the major groups like the Blind Boys both of Alabama and Mississippi, the Dixie Hummingbirds, Soul Stirrers, Pilgrim Jubilee, Salem Travelers, Harmonizing Four, Highway QC's, etc. We were there in our hometown of Chicago Heights at the Jones Memorial Community Center, on Sunday afternoon at DuSable, and Sunday night at the Baber Youth Center in

Gary, Indiana. The groups that Alex was in rehearsed at our house. I went to all of the other musicals I could find. Then before the sermons in church we had at least an hour of singing. I have heard great, good, bad, and ugly. I have seen competition in church—also politics.

What's a person to do when they are co-responsible for a church and is bone tired? I don't know if I want to hear another problem, pay another bill, talk to another creditor, hear another sermon or song, don't do it too long if you do, hear another pretty prayer. See another raggedly life.

I have become more comfortable with "rank" sinners. People who don't pretend—"take me as I am or not at all." People who will grow—if they want to—and let you know they are inching along and they are not talking on the mountains and being judgmental, being once removed from the streets and can't stand people who have not changed. Super spiritual folk drive me up the wall.

Those "blessed and highly favored of the Lord" irritate me. I know claiming and confession are important, but ramming it down someone's throat is nauseous. I am sounding cynical so I best quit for the day. I love God and I love people. And there are not buts. Maybe I am tired because I have so much stored up in me that needs to be shared. Maybe I am harboring too many sermons—too many songs.

I rested from writing two days. I went to church last night and I thoroughly enjoyed the lesson. Our church mother taught a lesson about people with different talents/gifts but the same spirit. There should be no competition between the hands and the feet because they have different functions. The comments from the listeners were refreshing. So you see I am not cynical about all church. Maybe that was the way I was feeling yesterday and tomorrow.

Today I thought about mothers. I wondered why there is such a connection between children and their moms. No matter how crummy we think the parent is, the child is tied to that person. Abandoned kids long for the mother. I imagined God standing somewhere on the golden streets surrounded by millions of unborn souls spanning from heaven to earth are millions of conduits.

There were eight hundred thousand conduits spanning from earth to God (some would get two or more souls). God chooses the proper mix for the conductor that would house and put flesh on His master pieces. As this soul is making its abode in the person chosen to be his mother, becoming flesh of her flesh and bone of her bone he is becoming one with her. What she eats or doesn't eat affects this person. I have noticed with my babies that they take on my habits. If I am cheerful while they are yet laying under my heart, they are happy babies. And vise versa.

When this carrier drinks, does dope, or smokes, the little person in most cases is affected in a negative way. You wonder why God didn't pass over that conduit. Then I think that God has set things in motion—His cycle of life, death and all the in betweens and He doesn't change—other than a miracle. This child living comfortably in its conduit's body getting instinct, conscious, feelings, hearing—when does the hearing start? I talked and sung to mine very early. I fell in love with them as soon as I knew I was pregnant. My arms protected my stomach from the beginning. So when does the bonding begin? I do know that some adopted children look for the person who carried them. Many long to feel the arms around them that may or may not have ever hugged them. They long to hear the voice they heard when they were nestled in safety. Even in adulthood most will get in a fetal position when things get extra tough. In their subconscious they remember their refuge—the womb. No worry, no care, everything they needed was provided and they were protected. I use God to cradle me when I'm fetal prone. There's a song we used to sing—you young people think you thought up our mother/father addressing God. If I haven't mentioned it, I am seventy years old. When I was a teenager we used to sing, "He's My Mother, He's My Father, He's My Sister, He's My Brother, He's My Everything!"

If anyone thought that was strange, they never said anything about it. Jesus said, "Jerusalem . . . how often would I have gathered you together as a hen gathers its chicks under her wings—but you would not." I let Him gather me. By day's end I'm ready to answer that summons. Also like Psalms 91 says—He will hide me in His pavilion. I run there often. One of our old songs is: In the shelter of the rock let me hide, or hide me in your love until the storms of life pass over.

A Mother's Love—when you are adopted, someone else was the conduit and another nurtured you. You had a wet nurse in many cases. That happened to the Christian church—we were grafted in and adopted. When God put you in a special carrier, the carrier had no choice (now they do make choices) but when you adopt a child, it is your choice and that child can feel special because they were chosen. When you fall and hurt yourself, it is your nurturer who kisses it and makes it better. The kiss of God is awesome. When I've brought my hurts to Him, I can feel

His embrace as a shield like a down comforter on a cold winter day. A mother would do whatever it takes in a positive way to insure her child's happiness.

I don't know what all I have told you, Simon, but today there are storm warnings and the birds are home. I can see at least twenty-five and that's from the branches I can see from the third floor balcony. I didn't see them when our temperature was 100 degrees plus. Of course I was so busy and hot that I didn't notice. We went to the prison that morning. We had 145 women. They put on extra guards because the number was so large. I am excited because it is not mandatory for them to come. Our team was missing several people. On the fifth Sunday we go in the morning and some of our team has other commitments on Sunday mornings. Husband played the piano, even though he had just gotten in Saturday night from Columbus, Ohio. He was tired but wouldn't miss the prison barring an emergency. We had communion and one of the inmates who was helping clean up gave me an idea. She drank about five of the leftover communion cups. We serve grape juice, not wine. I thought, "That might be one reason why we have many priests and pastors who are alcoholic." They empty the chalice filled with real wine. We don't use wine because we serve an undetermined amount of ex-alcoholics. I don't believe once an alcoholic, always one. No more than I believe that a murderer and liar can't change. I know that alcoholism is a disease, but so is an eating disorder, sexual addictions, cleptomania, etc. I have seen people delivered from all of the above, some through therapy and some through prayer. I would no more tempt an ex-alcoholic with wine/strong drink, than I would make a good person go bad by exposing them to their besetting problem. You must remember that these are my thoughts. I could be correct or not. It works for me. I will never become an alcoholic if I don't take the first drink. I come from a long line of drinkers on both sides of my family and I can imagine those genes just waiting to gobble up that drink and cry for more. So my addiction is food. Some people are addiction prone. I have seen "addicts" trade one addiction for another. So my drug of choice is food and laziness. I am not a glutton, I just don't exercise enough to work off the amount of calories I take in. I eat very healthy, but "enough dogs will down a bear!" Need I say more? Oh, just let me say that if I was consistent about not eating after seven I would lose weight. I like to reward myself just before bed with some drink like tea, juice or ginger ale with something that needs to be washed down. Sweets are not my thing, but cheese or something else salty—maybe peanut butter and Ritz will do the trick. I love pumpkin seeds—not sunflower. I used to eat mixed nuts (raw are good) or microwave popcorn. I got gastric reflux twice so now I just eat fruit. No fat—no reflux. No eating after seven—no gas. So I am working with my addiction. Since I like to chew and gum makes me bite my jaw, I buy cucumbers and use Bragg's apple cider vinegar, a little salt sense with pepper and chow away. Sometimes it's hard to find good cukes so I have learned to slice them lengthwise and scrape out the seeds. I am learning to use Splenda. Morning coffee I use half sugar and half Splenda. I use too much Coffee Mate. I just saw the fat content. Most of my meals are eaten without bread because if I eat bread, I want butter—not margarine or olive oil. I bought real popcorn yesterday and cooked it with olive oil and added no butter. It wasn't as tasty as the microwave or movie popcorn. If I had microwave popcorn I would eat a bag a day until it was gone. I will probably pop this corn once a month. That will save me some calories and my arteries will breathe a sigh of relief.

Going out to expensive restaurants began when we used the Happenings (entertainment) books as a fundraiser for the church. You buy one meal and get one free. I found some fantastic places. Many of them we started frequenting. I am not much of a meat eater, so I would order vegetables and take about two bites from my husband's steak. I very seldom fry at home—just fish. I bake, broil, or boil. I even read labels. Canned meats are a thing of the past. I buy Dairy Ease two percent milk. There are a few fruits I do not like, but I can't think of a vegetable that I can't tolerate. I love the cabbage family and all of the greens like collards, spinach, etc.

So somehow I will curtail my drug of choice. I am a good cook and can make a tasty meal out of a little of nothing. I need discipline, so I will do the nothing after dinner which should be seven o'clock, salty snacks, less fat including Coffee Mate, more water and more exercise. I can do all of this, but I need consistency and I want an exercise companion.

One of the reasons it is difficult to admit and conquer this demon is because you don't hurt anyone but yourself by eating. Maybe your family if you die from complications. My mom used to say, "People dig their graves with their teeth." Both of my parents died in their late sixties. Eating wrong was my mother's downfall and eating wrong, smoking and drinking were my father's. I should gather some strength, embrace discipline and latch on to some common sense so the rest of my life I can maintain the health I have and maybe improve upon it.

Have you ever noticed that you get all kinds of invitations to dine out when you are either fasting or have made a covenant with yourself to not diet but change your eating habits? I was offered Cheez-Its and Famous Amos cookies tonight. I could have said I will start the first thing in the morning so I compromised and took about ten Cheez-Its. I wasn't noble, I don't like chocolate chip cookies. They had no nuts! I will weight in tomorrow. I won't tell you how much. I will put it in a sealed envelope and each month I will check it and hopefully change it for a lower weight. This is August 2, 2006. So I am telling you, Simon, that I will lose some each month. I will set my goal for 20 pounds by Christmas.

Routine is so routine. I am so bored with the same "O." There was a song in grammar school that had a certain food for every day of the week. Sunday roast, don't remember Monday and Tuesday, but I think Wednesday was soup and Friday was fish. Then it asked is everybody happy? I am sick of cooking the same stuff. I think I will look in the cookbook and for two weeks cook something I have never tried before. I went to a Jewish wedding on Sunday and they served poached salmon. It was delicious. I have always said fish is the only thing I have to fry. I didn't give any other way a try. I have introduced my family to four new things in the last six months. Tea cakes, banana nut cake, pasta pie, and chicken wild rice casserole. They loved all of these. So I will find seven new recipes—maybe it will stimulate the other side of my brain and stop the boredom. I'll make each recipe last two days. I've had lamb chops in the freezer for several weeks. I haven't had the nerve to cook them. I tried a few decades ago and they weren't good. I did cook a leg of lamb for the holidays about ten years ago. It was eaten but must not have been spectacular because I never did it again.

I started again yesterday not eating after seven. I was going upstairs to exercise but the room is closed for remodeling. Just my luck. I need to start things when I am inspired until the habit takes over. I love the way I feel when I don't night eat. In fact it makes me want to sleep more—so I'm sleeping when I would be eating.

I wonder have I lived so long that my faith isn't up to par now. When I was younger I trusted God for everything and "He" worked for me. My prayers were answered, my needs were met, I was healthy. I didn't love God the way I do now, but I have allowed stress to invade my space. I counsel people who are sick and I don't go out on a limb like I used to, lay hands on, anoint with oil, pray and believe that it's taken care of. I sit in the hospital room with people and see their suffering and my heart breaks that I feel helpless. Maybe this started when my best friend had many medical problems but eventually had a brain tumor and after surgery went blind. Her livelihood was cut off. She and I were trusting God for her sight. She never smoked, drank, drugged—not around much second-hand smoke. I have known her to be a fair, pleasant Christian. I do know that God is able and that He forgives all our own inequities but LIFE is a booger and does not forgive. All the things we are exposed to that might cause us harm. Additives, microwaves, preservatives, tainted foods, to name a few things.

I was reading about the jelly fish which has two internal organs, a stomach and sex organs. Those are two things that destroy our bodies. We are digging our grave with our teeth and placing our bodies in these graves with our sex organs.

So life catches up with us and we can't blame God for choosing to go against the laws He has already set in motion—only at His discretion because He is sovereign.

There are several cases in the bible where prayer altered God's edit. Hezekiah turned his face to the wall and told him all of the positive things he had done. The same messenger that told him to set his house in order because he was going to die, came back and told him that God had added fifteen more years to his life. It makes you wonder what would have happened had Hezekiah not prayed. He could have just accepted his fate without a fight.

Many times we are just that accepting of a "life" decree and it happens. God has put "fight" in us and the more we use it, the more powerful it becomes. Look at the woman and the unjust judge. She knocked and knocked until he finally gave in to avenge her of her adversaries. Suppose she had taken the first no for her final answer—she would not have been avenged. She kept knocking/asking and the Judge granted her—her request.

I have known people applying for a job to keep checking on an opening after being told no. The person was seen or heard from so often that they were given a chance. I have known men who had first been rejected by a lady to finally "wear her down." Sometimes our commitment to the results we want wins out. Many times just being complacent and slothful we let our blessing slip through our fingers.

Simon, this might sound as if I am rambling. I have talked about divorce before. The subject is disturbing me today. We are having just as many divorces in the Christian world as in the non-Christian world. It would be interesting to see how Christians rate with other religions concerning divorce. The bible says God hates divorce. There are only two reasons given to divorce: One is adultery and the other is if the unbelieving spouse leaves. We have two Christians deciding to go their separate ways, not really caring that it will be traumatic for the kids. Ministers divorcing and still preaching that God can do anything. Why didn't He keep your marriage together? I am not the judge—but I can wonder, can't I? Should you divorce, the bible didn't say you could marry again. Will you spend the rest of your life without sex, or will you dabble on the side? Sex is no reason to stay in a marriage, but if you were as consistent with your marriage as you were about getting to the top of your field—getting that promotion, becoming that CEO. Praying for God's direction and when you arrived, your spouse wasn't in the equation. Neither was prayer and supplication. Since these are my thoughts, can I be as biased as I want to be? I don't even know if I feel this way. I don't know what I would do if I had to make that decision. We have gone through a lot in our marriage. For two years I didn't love him anymore. I say that, but I believe that once you love a person, if it was love not lust, it might be in a compartment of your heart, but it is still there.

During the time that the love was not evident because of what I was taught and what I believed and because I was a role model to some, I fasted, prayed and brought my body under subjection—the other parts of me followed suit. I don't say everyone will do the same because some have faith for their finances, or ministry, health, etc. that I might be lacking in. So I can't judge—I just wonder. I am so glad that God is God! He does His job without stressing out. Even though He did repent that He made mankind. Once Moses had to stand between Him and the people that had gone through the Red Sea because God would have killed them. Moses pleaded. The bible says, "Grieve not the Holy Spirit, so God has feelings. But His mercy endures forever."

My husband told me a story about this man who was always happy and telling people that situations could always be worse.

One day a man thought he had him so he said, "George, I had a dream about you. I dreamed you had died and gone to hell." George said,

"It could always be worse." The man asked how could anything be worse. George said, "It could be true."

It must make God happy to have someone loving and trusting Him so much. There is a song that our choir sings: "I want to say how much I love you in a very special way." I imagine God laughing and enjoying the praise. This is my imagination—let me do this.

Then I get sad because out of all the things He has done for me, I take Him for granted. He has blessed me with pain to know when something is wrong. How many people would get checked if they didn't feel pain?

How many times have I taken my brain for granted? Everything I have ever seen, heard, read, etc. is stored there somewhere. And my brain is less than a piece of sand on all the beaches of the world compared to the "All Knowing." When answers come to me, I have nerve enough to not just be happy, but to feel proud. God has put a little of Himself in each of us. He leads us and guides us if we listen to our conscience. I have overridden that God part of me so much that there are times when I've traveled the low road—the crowded road—not the one less traveled.

I think of the hearts I've broken in my lifetime, the people I have disappointed, but I learned I am a different person. If I had known better, I would have done better. I have always desired to be a better person. I measure myself often to see if I have grown, see if I am learning from my mistakes, check my motives after my actions. I never measure up to my expectations of myself but I thank God that it could always be worse. I could be on a downward spiral.

Simon II—September 28, 2007

I just had a long discussion with husband concerning the retreat I am on. I am really disturbed about the church and I have decided to do what I do best when things are out of whack in my opinion. When things are moving in a negative behavior, I get a feeling of dread. I can feel my blood cruising in my veins. I feel very unsociable—me who is a social butterfly—I feel like screaming if I hear one more complaint or hear another "put down" of someone else. I am miserable. I know that I need to remove myself from situations. So I go on a shut in or a retreat.

I must commend the Catholic Church in Minnesota. They have several retreat places for burned out pastors. Some with scholarships. This is my second attempt to go. Last year my husband was called away to a meeting. I thought we both shouldn't be away at the same time—especially if we hadn't planned the time away. So I have had this feeling for quite a while. I suppressed it and went on functioning at three-fourths my normal self.

This time I was forced to go in somewhere. I talked with several of the retreat spaces. One was very rustic, porta potty, no running water, dining room about a block away, etc. There were some with beautiful settings on the St. Croix, others with nice dorms, etc. I made the decision to stay at home with no phone and minimal communication. I need to do what I do best when I am in trouble—pray and commune with God. I needed some questions answered. How do I fit in the mix? Am I contributing to the chaos? What can I do to help the matter? Give me wisdom to deal with the things that are going on.

Let me see if I can recap the things that have happened this year as I see it.

A minister's wife gave him a month's notice that she was leaving him—and she did. I am not going to address blame because only God knows for sure. I do know that she was much younger than he and he was overprotective or possessive. She liked skating and other young things and he wanted church and home and wanted her to do the same.

The wife had friends at the church and they seemingly took sides. We didn't know any negative things about either that would hinder either one of them from functioning in the church. Unless I overtake them in a fault how could I sit them down. She was faithful to the church and so was he. The three kids were the ones who were suffering. The wife has female friends in the church who sympathized with her, so with her husband's "old" ways, they didn't like him either. He was truly wounded and would talk about his wounds to anyone who would listen. The thing that bothered me was how adults talk everything in front of their children and expect them to respect authority.

Then some of the friends fell out with each other. When one did something in the church, the other one wouldn't support it. One obviously took the low road and the other one agonized over it. Other people see this action or hear about it and leave the church because they had junk in the streets.

I am reminded of the "jumping carp" fish that were coming up the Mississippi River jumping in boats and growing larger each month because they were feeding on the native fish in the river and on the game fish in the lakes. It was like the church had a ceiling where it wouldn't/couldn't grow past a certain stage.

I have to find a way to break through this dam. So husband was saying this morning that he was preaching the word and living a consistent life. I wasn't accusing him for how I am feeling. I just told him that he gave some apostles, pastors, teachers, etc. all for the perfecting of the saints.

That's why I need to be alone with the Lord. He knows where I am and where I want Him to take me. I know there is nothing too hard for Him. I am different in my thinking. I believe in holiness. I believe that falling in love with the Lord will help you walk worthy in the vocation where you are called—that you made a commitment to God and each other, that you would stay with this marriage. If it is something that you can't live with, you can leave but fast and pray that God will fix the situation. Many people go into marriage seeing a light at the end of the tunnel. But you can't be doing that dating other people. The lesser of the two evils would be to divorce. Both are evil—divorcing or dating while yet married. Oh, well, I won't get into that because every tub must sit on its own bottom. Everyone is responsible for their own deeds. I don't have a heaven or hell to put anyone in.

I read Psalms 17:17,18: Unless the Lord has been my help, my soul would soon have settled in silence. If I say "my foot slips," your mercy, oh Lord, will hold me up.

I cried when I read this because it described how I was feeling. I love God and I feel close to Him. My heart has been "fed up" with the church I helped to organize. I am the co-founder. It was the prison team that I formed who were our first members. I found the church for thirteen years that we worshipped in and my friend incorporated us and did our 501c3. I had a co-worker draw our logo. I started the newsletters, rap sessions, the feedings, etc. Now I am dreading to go to church. So you say it's a spirit. Be as it may—that is why I am on this retreat. I have completely put myself at the mercy of the court of heaven and God in particular.

You see I remember the church where I grew up in being an anointed church. I don't mean just shouting, I mean people getting delivered. Folks come in high on drugs or high on alcohol and leave delivered. I have seen many miracles. Now we see them mostly medical. We didn't have the technology, so we relied on God. He didn't let us down. We trusted Him for our livelihood. We didn't have welfare and emergency assistance. We didn't have the luxury of suing everyone for infractions. We were going to pray for this lady on crutches and she asked us not to until after she had won her lawsuit. She knew that God was a healer. I don't know if she got anything from the lawsuit. Was she really hurt? What were her motives? But she knew/believed that if prayer was offered, she would be healed. That's the kind of church I grew up in. That everyone was expected to live right. By the rules. Even if the rules weren't accurate, we obeyed them. I have never worn a pair of pants in my life. Our church preached against women wearing pants, lipstick, movies, dancing, too much TV, drinking, smoking, double marriages, and you name it.

At about 55 years of age I discovered that pants were not the clothes worn when this was written but I hadn't worn pants by this age so why break a record. I am very selective about movies. Maybe one every other year. My TV watching is limited also. Maybe our church was too strict, but we had time to meditate and pray. Consequently we had "power." Not all—some folk are just lazy and don't want to think for themselves. They wouldn't dare read anything other than the bible, not even an encyclopedia or bible commentary or history to see if the interpretations are right.

If people were jealous of each other, they would be ashamed to let others know that they were that petty. We stood up and testified at every service. We had to speak to our salvation. Have we lived our best today? If not, we went to the altar for prayer. I am sure we made a platform for hypocrites—people who got up and said the speech out of habit or because of expectations. We only have a few "burning" testimonies at our church. People telling of prayers answered or other blessings, near accidents, job promotions, etc.

So I don't remember all of this stuff in church. Maybe I was too young (from 10-31). Maybe older people protected us from the negatives. We found out things on our own—like when a very strict, very emotional elder and his wife came to our church. He was made assistant pastor. He could really preach and he could hold the young people's attention. He would be talking about the Lord while driving and take his hands off the wheel to praise God. Or I have seen him pull the car over to the side of the road, get out and dance on the side of the road.

I have found that overly emotional people are that way in many cases—the first to get angry, jealous, lustful and so on. Anyway, this preacher had left a wife and five children in Mississippi and he wasn't even married to the woman he was with. That's why it is important for us to lead you to Christ and nurture you but keep your focus on Him. Tell them to follow you (we are examples and role models) as you follow Christ. When we stop following Christ, you stop following us. Our duty as we do our natural children is to nurture them to a normal growth rate—allowing them to sit upon their own, crawl, walk and run. We know they will need to be potty trained. With studying the word of God and building a healthy spiritual relationship they will learn that the accidents will be fewer and farther apart—until one day they will seldom hare an "accident."

So I learned with this emotional preacher and his wife not to judge a person's spirituality by how vocal or animated they are.

So, Simon, I didn't need you then. I had several friends and many spiritual sisters and brothers to talk with. I can't remember us gossiping, but let's be real, we were teenagers and the grapevine was alive and well. We respected adults and we didn't let them see us talking in a negative way.

We had one person who prayed folks' business. Lord, help Lester with his lust problem, help Angela stop smoking, and Lord, Sarah is pregnant (as if he didn't know) so help her marry the boy. It was fun praying with the gossip. We found out all of the church's business. Well, that stopped abruptly after the higher ups got wind of this.

Simon, all and all I had a great experience at church. When I was young I had a good support group of people who even though from different backgrounds shared the same values. I was happy on Tuesdays, Thursdays and Fridays because I would be at church with my church family. We studied the bible and competed with each other—who could explain what we studied. Who would give the summary. We never knew who would. So we were all alert. We learned public speaking in church. We were encouraged to sing and pray. It was an unspoken law that we were involved in most of the ministries.

The sanctuary was respected. Treats were only for small children. We didn't have children's church unless you called Sunday school and evening bible class children's church. We had junior church on Thursday night and also choir rehearsal. But the children sat through Tuesday, Friday and Sunday morning and Sunday night services with their parents. Our pastor told us to bring the kids even if they went to sleep because it would get into their subconscious.

We didn't get into a lot of negative behavior because we were otherwise occupied. I can't remember any girl having a baby out of wedlock or any boy going to jail in our group. We had a few "seven" months babies, but their parents were married. There were no divorces in our church when

I was growing up. We had people who came to the church with a couple of mates behind them, but after they "got saved," they remained married.

One man came to our home town and later to our church because I witnessed to him. After the powers that be discovered he had been married, they advised he send for his wife. They had been separated for quite a while. He did and she wreaked havoc in his life, in the church and caused a friend of hers to have a nervous breakdown by blatantly flirting with her husband while the wife was pregnant. Finally the man knew that his first decision to leave her was the right one for him. He divorced her, went to another state, remarried, studied for the ministry and became a pastor. His former wife married several times and was separated from her last husband last I heard.

So what about divorce? Personally I believe God can fix any situation, marriage included. When I was young I heard of people in another strict religion that they could get forgiveness for murder, but not divorce. That just never made any sense to me. I can't find a spot in my brain to accept that God forgives some sins and not others. We categorize sin. I might be a chronic liar and you might be divorced one time. The bible said a liar wouldn't even tarry in His sight. He is going to judge the whoremonger and adulterer. Don't ask me to explain this in theological terms, but in my layman's understanding it makes sense to me that the heart of a liar is deceitful and he would take any chance to take advantage of a situation, that his motives might be selfish and many sins might be encompassed in this one act of sin; whereas a divorce might be just one act.

I do not advocate divorce, and I wonder why there are more divorces now than in years past. Maybe because people are living longer than before. We are exposed to more people and have something to compare our lives to. People didn't know there was more to life than a domineering spouse. They couldn't see the changing trends. People didn't see greener pastures. Most things were equal. Most people went to some sort of religious establishment. And staying in a marriage was taught. It was expected and in some cases enforced by society, church and family. The female for the most part was dependent on the man. She had limited employable skills so she stayed whether she was happy or not. Maybe she didn't know what happiness was. They were expected to stay until death separated them and they did. Commitment was more important than love and passion. Many of the families that were started were both virgins. Now it seems rare that either are. Some can be classified technically as virgins because oral sex and heavy petting is becoming acceptable to many so these potential spouses have too many partners to compare their mates to. Or commitment to a promise of fidelity doesn't mean as much to some as it did in years past. We went from stoning to the scarlet letter, to acceptance and understanding. I remember when adultery was a crime; mates had to have actual proof to get a divorce. Detectives were hired and pictures were taken as proof. People could be sued for alienation of affection. "You took my husband or wife." I content that no one can "take" them away and if so, would you want someone so weak and stupid that they could be "taken away?" Thinking, praying could be done before ending a relationship. The bible says no "person" goes on a journey without first setting down and counting up the cost.

Make a plan. Don't let anyone cripple you—they pay all the bills, drive the car, etc. You can be independently dependent. I might allow you to do this for me and I might like it, but I can do it for myself. I refuse to stop learning. Books are my friend. I watch the news, read books for dummies. Things I don't know in my interest, I get a how to book.

I seek out friends from other countries and cultures so if my husband dies before me, I keep myself marketable. So what can I do at 71? I can consult, I'm a good cook, in good health so I can cater. I do seminars and workshops. Only as I want to, but if it was a matter of livelihood, I could do more.

Maybe the lowest paid person in the marriage is threatened with a feeling of insecurities. I know some people making extra money selling products and services. Prepaid Legal is one of the going things now. Can you play the piano, or any other instrument? Teach the instrument. You might have just finished book two. Teach what you know. Voice? Can you help someone learn English? To read? Can you shop for someone? Read for the visually challenged? Clean an apartment? Wash? Maybe these are not dignified enough for you, but it isn't dignified to have someone call you and your phone is disconnected, or your car has been repossessed, you lose your house or apartment. It is more dignified than sleeping around for money. I'm laughing because I don't think you should sleep around period.

Before I retired I worked with people who told me they had a pimp. I thought to myself, if I was going to do the work, I was going to keep the money.

One lady who was 39 had a husband who was 55. He had not had sex with her in almost two years. Her account was: he started sleeping on the couch. When she came downstairs, he went up and vice versa. She felt rejected. After much talking and begging she started talking to others about it. A preacher started counseling her, talking to her for hours at a time. The husband didn't like it but he didn't try to stop it by wooing his wife.

Long and short she told husband she was leaving if things didn't change. It didn't change and she left. Not for the minister but I think he gave her courage to do so. She and child slept on the floor in her brother's empty house. She was there for a few weeks until she found a two-bedroom apartment in the worst part of the ghetto. I am so pro-family and anti-divorce that this put me in a funk. My heart bled for the family and especially the daughter who hurt very vocally in front of the church. Whenever there was a song, testimony or prayer that spoke to the situation, she wailed. Our hearts were broken. After their break up, most of our couples left the church. One said, "If your marriage fails, there is no hope for ours!"

The first couple had been married for eighteen years. Our church went from a couples' church to a church that had only a few married couples. We were a church that called a couple by name—Jacob and Rachel, Rose and Daniel, etc. Maybe they left our church so the "spirit" of divorce wouldn't overtake them. Maybe they felt we could/should have been harder on them and "made" them stay together. The female who left went to a larger church in the suburbs for healing. The saints really judged her. I thought if we prayed and loved them, that eventually they would reunite. The problem would be if either chose to remarry. We had one couple at the beginning of our church who separated but never divorced. After nineteen years they went back together. So I had hope. We had never been pastors before and this was our first encounter with divorce in the church among leaders.

There must be standards. Can a person just quit a person because they are tired of them or see someone else they think might be better for them?

Since we don't actually see what is going on in the house, "no matter how thin the slice of bread, it still has two sides." If we disallow a divorced person from ministering in the church, we would have very few musicians, choir members, deacons, ministers, ushers, prayer leaders, Sunday school teachers and youth leaders. The bible says let the wheat and tare grow together and he would separate when he returns.

When we see something that looks like tare and it might be wheat and vice versa. The roots are so intertwined that you can pull up a tare and because the roots are wrapped around the wheat, you will pull up the good with the undesirable.

So, Simon, what's a person to do? Are there any rules other than the Ten Commandments that are absolute?

Then the bible says that there are two commandments—to love God with all of our hearts and to love your neighbor as yourself. Where are grace and mercy? Are we taking advantage of the blood of Jesus? Do we crucify Him afresh by living undisciplined lives?

If we fasted and prayed more and sought His face, if we panted after Him like a thirsty deer panteth after the water brook, if we reckoned ourself dead or died daily, could we stay dead? Our, as my mentor said when she had dragged herself to the coffin and gotten in, one of her parts would come alive. Before she knew it her arm fell out of the coffin, when she had gotten that back in her leg would fall out. Then when everything was properly enclosed, her eyes would pop open. She let me know that it was and is a constant job.

So if this is true, what is the difference between a saint and a sinner? Can I just come to the altar, give my heart to the Lord and return to life as usual? Should I care? Should I dip? Whose servants are they anyway?

Is it my responsibility to just preach the gospel and let "every tub sit on its own bottom?" Every organization must have rules. They are fired if they break the rules at work. What are we to do at church? Are we to have more compassion than a workplace, or fraternity, or a club? Are we to accept any kind of raggedy living? What are we to teach our children about values and morals if it can all hang out. No boundaries?

Do I gag at a gnat and swallow a camel as the bible says?

I might see a divorcee or smoker who exemplifies all of the fruits of the spirit or a person who has one mate, doesn't drink, smoke, or chew, and can't get along with anyone, mean and evil, who would I choose? I think the smoker or divorcee (don't know the masculine tense).

We sang at the church conference where the denomination was voting on ordaining gay pastors. Some of our "saints" thought themselves too "good" to support this organization, even though they were once removed from dope, prostitution, prison, grand theft, etc. It didn't dawn on them that they could have been there to encourage the ones who voted against this ordinance and were hurting because they had to vote against people in their families and dear friends. Most of them were hurt—they all needed comfort and compassion.

Our gospel songs lighten the day. They responded to "hold on, help is on the way."

Don't give up on God because you aren't "there" yet. If you are sincere, God will get you there.

Since God is sovereign He can do whatever He wants to do mingled with mercy. Look at Romans 2:11-15. The bible says that God has put a little of himself in each person. If a person has not heard of Him but acts according to the dictates of their conscious, they will be saved. Not only is God sovereign, but He is merciful and fair. So I spend no time trying to judge "another man's servants." The bible says it is before Him (God) that the person stands or falls. Not before me.

So I don't spend much time trying to legislate "choice." I might not have but ten million times to breathe so I don't plan to waste any of that breath on things I can't do anything about. God gave people the privilege of choice. Why are we taking that right away—that God given right? We know there is a road that takes us to negative places and a road to take us to a positive place. "If you want to kill a dog you can always find a stick." We can legislate abortion, but we cannot stop it. Rich people have always been able to have abortions, and many poor people had them also, many times by butchers.

We can and should make laws, but I don't think we as Christians should spend a lot of time picketing because a majority of "Christians" are agreeing to kill babies in Iraq. Thou shalt not kill should be across the board.

Simon, did I tell you about Ruby #1 and Ruby #2?

Husband says, "I should have followed my first mind!"

Well, my first mind, Ruby #1, is a bad girl. She isn't even saved. She is not dignified or refined. She will tell you where to get on and off.

She hates preliminaries that go on and on. Don't repeat the same words in a song for too long. You already said that in a prayer or testimony. Don't call her and she has to do the talking. When the conversation is over, let's not just breathe on the phone.

One day in church a preacher had preached in and out of the bible about twenty minutes. Then he said, "I just don't know what else to say." Well Ruby #1 said in her mind, "Just shut the f _ _ _ up!"

We went out after church—even with the preacher—and I told them what #1 thought. They laughed so hard because she admitted what they all were thinking. Even the preacher had to laugh.

I thought about how people would always put me up to saying and doing their dirty work. You ask the teacher, parent, mothers of the church and so on!

Paul in the bible said when he would do good, evil was ever present. He had two natures. #1 is my negative nature. But as Ruby #2 began to grow, #1 got smaller. My theory about the glass half full and half empty is: The half empty is the negatives—so how do I get rid of the negatives? Fill up the glass with positives and it leaves little or no room for negatives.

So Ruby #2 is dominate. She is the voice of reason. She is saved and loves the Lord. She has class. Sometimes she has to laugh at how ridiculous #1 can be. She as #1 is hilarious at times.

#2 fell in love with the Lord. I don't know where or when—it was gradual. It was not love at first sight. I had a crush or infatuation, but I fooled around and fell in love. So I endeavor doing the things that please Him. I started to say "try" but husband says, "trying is lying!"

I was surprised when #1 thought that foul word. Didn't know it was in me. I had to quit a job once because the CEO was so foul mouthed. Those words were forever in the front of my mind. I had to think before I spoke. "Evil communication corrupts good manners." I guess #1 retained a few.

Did I tell you that I am tired?

I put an ad in the neighborhood paper asking to share a church facility in 1977. I think we were one of the first to do so in Minnesota. April of that year we had our first service at 2639 Thomas North. We were there for 13 years.

We went to 2119 Lyndale Avenue North under contract for deed. When the balloon payment came due, we had no money. Marie mortgaged her house to pay it and that gave us several years (about six) to pay her off. We had several businesses and others to cheat us. We knew how to get people saved and delivered, get them back into society, but we had no knowledge of legal stuff. So we panelled the church. They half finished the job and sued us for the money. We went to court. They went out of business and sold the debt to another businessman who took the church from us. One day before the final sale the Lord sent an investor who kept the church for two years—we could still use the church and pay utilities. Then they sold it back to us for $1.00. They tried to buy the lot next door so we could expand, but the city wouldn't sell.

The Lord sent us many more angels during those trying times. WCCO did a segment on us which brought in several thousand dollars. The state under Attorney General Hatch helped us with a class action suit. It will take many years to recoup some things ($180.00) a year.

We have a dentist who husband met at a wedding who saw his teeth and donated him "some teeth" which he left in Detroit. He did it again and we almost left them again. The maid had them on her tray when we rushed back to the hotel.

Our choir had a yearly revival at Shakopee Women's Facility. He lost them again. We had the employees looking all over. Finally he found them days later in his pockets. Subconsciously I think he didn't want them.

Our primary doctor cam several times and because our church was "frail" and we had so many animated people he told us that after going downstairs to the bathroom that he knew the angels were holding up the floor where the beams were being pressed to their limits as the people were dancing and keeping time with the excellent music.

During those times we had people who came to use us. One signed husband's name on a marriage certificate while he was in prison. He came to the church when he got out. Brought a lady and her children to church on Sunday. She came to the altar. By Tuesday she was dead. Tied to the bed with her children and set afire. He got three life sentences.

One guy went to St. Paul and got beaten up by a Spanish guy. Came home, got a gun and shot the first Spanish guy he saw. He got life.

When 2119 got too frail to worship in after many mishaps and so-called benefactors, we went to Christ English at 3210 Oliver North. They have been great to us.

Our goal is to repair 2119 and still keep 3210.

We have found that some of our people like the church in the hood more than stained glass windows and good fellowship halls.

The music was so good and so loud and so long that Ruby #1 got impatient sometimes and the people would hang their heads out of the bus windows to hear it. That little church was so full that the ushers would turn people away. Husband told them never turn anyone away—even if they had to sit in the bathroom stall.

Our neighbor"hood" people didn't follow us to the new location. Whenever we got to our wits' end God would send us an angel—a shot in the arms.

Charlene, Garcia, Fox, Sandstone Prison, then our spiritual sons, Ford, Anderson, Brown, Shanks, Campbell, Flannigan, our sister churches, Kevin and Jim, Curtis, sometimes calls from our "children" across the country, Yadira, Rohini, Shetaze, Mirtha, Magda. The ones who are here in town and at UDT have been a real help. I love them all.

Where are we going from here? Hopefully to beautify 2119 and have many services there and to yet have the 2 p.m. services along with weddings and funerals at 3210.

Simon, I will be satisfied with any outcome as long as God is in control. God has never failed me. I have had many more good days than bad. I've had more happiness than sorrow. There's even peace in my valleys. Sometimes I have to go into my quiet space, but when I come out I am equipped. I have promised people that I will never be moody. Whenever they see me I will be pleasant. When I feel I can't do that, they won't see me until I can get it together. So far I have kept that promise.

Good night, Simon, until next time.